The Vow of the Ikeda Kayo-kai

ENCOURAGEMENT FOR YOUNG WOMEN

SGI President Daisaku Ikeda and his wife, Kaneko Ikeda, upon their first visit to the Soka Young Women's Center in Shinanomachi, Tokyo, June 4, 2009. (June 4 is now celebrated as World Ikeda Kayo-kai Day.)

The following is inscribed on a plaque accompanying the lyrics for "Cherry Blossoms of Youth":

At our mentor-disciple castle on Mount Soka
The treasured cherry tree
Blooms in full glory in the lives of our young women

How remarkable that a new generation's acceptance of the pledge to imbue
     society with Buddhist ideals in 1978
Took place on March 16
And in the castle of the Buddhist Law in Tachikawa
Illuminated by the spirit of justice
A poem — "Cherry Blossoms of Youth" — was born
Would a stormy vortex of the three formidable enemies
Then descend upon the Soka Gakkai, whose adherents have practiced according
     to the Buddha's teachings?

Nichiren, the one and eternal Buddha of the Latter Day of the Law, writes,
"The graceful cherry blossoms come forth from trees…
Fortune comes from one's heart and makes one worthy of respect" (WND-I, 1137)
Heavenly maidens, with hearts like exquisite cherry blossoms
Raise their melodious voices courageously in song, in unison with their mentor
And even in the trials of darkest winter, they triumph with bright cheer

In the fullness of time, the Kayo community in the essential phase
Will spread throughout the entire world
Scattering its blossoms of Mentor-Disciple cherry blossoms, Friendship cherry
     blossoms, Happiness cherry blossoms, and Peace cherry blossoms
We pray for our beloved daughters' progress
Toward eternal happiness and enlightenment
As they walk and bear witness on the flowery path of the glorious victory of
     Buddhism's propagation
And with this wish, we erect in the Hall of Hope this inscription of "Cherry
     Blossoms of Youth"

     Daisaku and Kaneko Ikeda
     May 3, 2009

President and Mrs. Ikeda stroll through the Soka Young Women's Center, viewing the inscription of the poem, "Cherry Blossoms of Youth."

The Soka Young Women's Center opened on May 3, 2006.

President Ikeda plays "Sakura" and "Dainanko" on the piano
for the Ikeda Kayo-kai members, June 4, 2009.

Soka Gakkai young women sing "The Vow of the Ikeda Kayo-kai,"
June 4, 2009.

見つめなむ
妙法蓮華の
蓮の花

大切な大切な我らが
宝の花に贈る

二〇〇九年六月四日

President Ikeda's photo and poem to the young women's division:

I am watching over you,
my lotus flowers of Myoho-renge

To my most precious daughters, the young women's division
June 4, 2009

World Ikeda Kayo-kai inaugural meeting on September 5, 2008,
at the Soka Young Women's Center.

DAISAKU IKEDA

The Vow of the Ikeda Kayo-kai

ENCOURAGEMENT FOR YOUNG WOMEN

World Tribune Press

Published by World Tribune Press
606 Wilshire Blvd.
Santa Monica, CA 90401

© 2011 Soka Gakkai

ISBN 978-1-935523-09-3

Cover and interior design by Scribe Typography

All rights reserved

Printed in the United States of America

10 9 8 7 6 5 4 3 2 1

Contents

Editor's Note

"Kayo-kai" literally means "Flower-Sun Group." This was the name of a young women's division training group formed by second Soka Gakkai president Josei Toda in 1952. It also refers to the Ikeda Kayo-kai, a young women's division group formed at the proposal of SGI President Daisaku Ikeda. The latter group was first established in Japan in commemoration of the fiftieth anniversary of Kosen-rufu Day, March 16, 2008, with the SGI Ikeda Kayo-kai later being inaugurated on September 5, 2008. The group comprises all active young women's division members. In Japanese, the name "Ikeda Kayo-kai" is often abbreviated as "Kayo-kai," or simply "Kayo."

Also, President Ikeda sometimes uses the pen name, Shin'ichi Yamamoto (see the essays that start on p. 55 and 79).

The following abbreviations appear in some citations:

GZ, page number(s)	refers to *Nichiren Daishonin gosho zenshu* (*The Collected Writings of Nichiren Daishonin*), the Japanese-language compilation of Nichiren Daishonin's writings (Tokyo: Soka Gakkai, 1952)
LSOC, page number(s)	refers to *The Lotus Sutra and Its Opening and Closing Sutras,* translated by Burton Watson (Tokyo: Soka Gakkai, 2009)
OTT, page number(s)	refers to *The Record of the Orally Transmitted Teachings,* the compilation of Nichiren's oral teachings on the Lotus Sutra; translated by Burton Watson (Tokyo: Soka Gakkai, 2004)
WND-1 and WND-2	refer to *The Writings of Nichiren Daishonin,* volumes 1 and 2 respectively (Tokyo: Soka Gakkai, 1999 [vol. 1] and 2006 [vol. 2])

Foreword

The Ikeda Kayo-kai is a young women's training group established by SGI President Ikeda in September 2008. It is a network of young women who—by living the guidance of their cherished mentor, President Ikeda, deepening their faith through studying Nichiren Daishonin's writings, and creating friendships with one another—strive to become young women of confidence and conviction who can triumph over any challenge.

On September 5, 2008, more than 250 young women from around the world gathered at the Soka Young Women's Center in Tokyo for the inaugural World Ikeda Kayo-kai. In his message, President Ikeda described the significance of this group: "Nichiren Daishonin declares that women open the gateway (see WND-2, 884). Today's gathering of wise young women leaders from around the globe represents the opening of an exciting new door to a hope-filled era of worldwide kosen-rufu—one that will continue into the eternal future. . . . I close this message with my fervent prayer that the members of the SGI Ikeda Kayo-kai—my daughters and successors who are eternally one in spirit with me—will always shine with hope, good fortune, and wisdom, and be rigorously protected by the benevolent functions of the universe" (see pp. 109–12). The representatives who attended this meeting returned home invigorated with their determination to expand the network of the Ikeda Kayo-kai in their respective countries.

The original Kayo-kai was formed by second Soka Gakkai president Josei Toda on October 21, 1952. Twenty young women met with President Toda twice a month to discuss topics ranging from Nichiren Buddhism and the spirit of the Soka Gakkai to literature, politics, economics, and art. In *The Human Revolution,* President Ikeda writes: "The former Kayo-kai members would fondly look back upon those days, the precious memories vivid in their hearts. Without that training, they wouldn't have been able to cultivate the lives they came to enjoy. They might have followed some obscure, entirely different path. Throughout their lives they cherished seeds of guidance they had received as members of this special group—seeds that grew and blossomed in whatever circumstance they found themselves" (pp. 900–01).

As we commemorate the sixtieth anniversary of the foundation of the young women's division this year (2011), it is with great pride and joy that we publish this English-language edition of *The Vow of the Ikeda Kayo-kai* with messages, essays, and a speech by President Ikeda. It is intended to help young women lead lives brimming with happiness and victory based on the spirit of the oneness of mentor and disciple with President Ikeda.

Preface

Joyfulness is one of life's mysteries, according to Simone Weil, the French philosopher. Where may we find the wellspring of this joy? The conclusion she reached was that joyfulness cannot come from a source external to the individual or group. It is something that must come welling up from inside.

Our young women of the Soka Gakkai shine with a radiant joy emanating from the life force of their precious youth, like the blazing red glow of the morning sun. These flowers of peace and happiness bloom vibrantly and magnificently day after day.

Many extraordinary women, such as Simone Weil, have enriched the world throughout history. If they were to view the procession of hope by the group whose name, *Kayo,* stands for flowers and sunshine, I am sure that they would rise to give them a round of joyous and thunderous applause.

It is entirely appropriate that the book *The Vow of the Ikeda Kayo-kai* was published on this joyous occasion of the eightieth anniversary of the founding of the Soka Gakkai (2010, the Japanese edition). I join my wife, a member of the first graduating class, in offering our sincerest congratulations.

The jubilant Soka spirit of community spreads throughout the world, accompanied by the dynamism and ever-present, cheerful smiles of the members of the young women's division.

The dance of the youthful Kayo members promulgates the Buddhist teachings all over the world—to large countries, newly established countries, countries with multiethnic populations—and becomes a bright source of hope for many people. This truly makes my heart dance and fills me with happiness.

In the long-suffering, war-scarred country of Cambodia, the Ikeda Kayo-kai was formed in November 2008. I first visited that unforgettable country in 1961, the year after becoming the third president of the Soka Gakkai. Next year (2011), we will celebrate the tenth anniversary since the incorporation of our activities there.

In that cherished land, with which I feel an affinity, one young woman became the driving force that helped nurture a group of peace-loving young women, lovely fragrant flowers. This intelligent young woman became a member of the Soka Gakkai International in the United States on September 1, 2001, just ten days before the horrific terrorist attacks of September 11, 2001. In the midst of the subsequent global maelstrom of distrust and hatred, she keenly felt the importance of dialogue among civilizations. Consequently, with firm resolve, she entered Soka University of America.

Together at the university with good friends from all around the world, she grew and developed day by day, and the philosophy of peace and human rights became impressed upon her heart. The young woman returned to her motherland, Cambodia, after graduation, expanding the reach of Kayo groups for young women. She is now still contributing valiantly to her society.

Currently, I am conducting a dialogue with Dr. Sarah Ann Wider, the president of The Ralph Waldo Emerson Society and a leading American poet.

Dr. Wider commented that the term *jiyu*, to spring from the earth, teaches us to extend our roots deep into the soil. It teaches us the importance of not turning away from our present reality but of doing good deeds in the place where we find ourselves.

When one woman rises up passionately and courageously to pursue her calling with her entire being, her community and the entire region begin to change. She sparks a tangible shift in the consciousness of the times. We can see evidence of this in many instances in history.

Henrik Ibsen, a Norwegian playwright, wrote that one person has the ability to shine the light of hope and grace on many people and also that the intention and determination of one person can make many great things possible. Ibsen was a great writer whose works my mentor, Josei Toda, chose to use as educational material for the Kayo-kai, the young women's division leadership development group that he founded.

Kayo was the name Mr. Toda originally gave to the young women's division. The name crystallizes his prayers for the young women, that is, that they may be as lovely as a flower and radiate a sense of honor and dignity as bright as the sun.

Further, the word *kayo* is related to one of Mr. Toda's favorite Chinese heroes, Zhuge Liang. It is a place name in Xian Province in the southwestern region of China. More specifically, it is another name for the Kingdom of Shu, which was closely associated with Zhuge Liang.

Kayo is also the name of a Chinese classic of regional history—*Hua yang guo zhi* (The History of Kayo Kingdom)—whose legendary tales celebrate the exploits of many courageous women in the region who were unrivaled in all of China.

All of the beloved daughters of the noble Kayo-kai are exuberant and extraordinary heroines whose names will surely be recognized as outstanding adherents in the history of kosen-rufu.

I earnestly hope that each and every one of these dear heavenly maidens, intent on her precious mission, will be wrapped in an eternal embrace of happiness and prosperity. In honor of our mentor, with whom my wife and I were inseparable, we offer our sincere prayer.

I always keep by my side the work *Contemporary Japanese Translation of the Writings of Nichiren Daishonin*, which is a crystallization of intensive research and study by our dear members in the Educational Affairs Department of the young women's division. One passage I would like to mention is from a letter titled "The Real Aspect of the Gohonzon": "Never seek this Gohonzon outside yourself. The Gohonzon exists only within the mortal flesh of us ordinary people who embrace the Lotus Sutra and chant Nam-myoho-renge-kyo. The body is the palace of the ninth consciousness, the unchanging reality that reigns over all of life's functions" (WND-I, 832).

Courage, wisdom, compassion, hope, conviction, endurance—the source of all our power and determination to progress toward happiness lies within ourselves. Indeed, the very lives of the Soka young women are the embodiment of the venerable essence of the Buddha.

In *The Record of the Orally Transmitted Teachings,* Nichiren Daishonin clarifies this concept: "This passage refers to the great joy that one experiences when one understands for the first time that one's mind from the very beginning has been the Buddha" (OTT, 211–12).

Like the pure and noble white lotus, may you advance in the name of justice with the sacred pledge in your heart. May you live each day victoriously with no regrets, just as the sun rises in the morning sky.

This preface expresses my deepest and most fervent prayer: May our precious and beloved daughters of the young women's division walk proudly and confidently on the path of the greatest of all joys that humankind has been seeking.

Daisaku Ikeda
October 2, 2009

Speech

At a young women's division gathering held on June 4, 2009, at the Soka Young Women's Center in Shinanomachi, Tokyo, on the occasion of SGI President and Mrs. Ikeda's first visit to the center, which opened on May 3, 2006.

Live the Five Eternal Guidelines

I am overjoyed to finally visit the Soka Young Women's Center, something I have long wanted to do. My wife, in particular, as the center's honorary director, is chanting Nam-myoho-renge-kyo for the young women who look after this beautiful palace of good fortune and wisdom, as well as for all those who gather here from throughout Japan and the world. For some time now, she has been saying that she wanted to take up your kind invitation to us and visit the center at the earliest possible date. Thank you for inviting us! And congratulations! I would also like to thank the center's caretakers for all their hard work.

Today's gathering was organized with short notice, so only representatives are present, but just now my wife and I chanted earnestly for the good health and happiness of all our young women's division members. Indeed, we do so every morning and evening. Please give our warmest regards to those we couldn't meet today.

Like Flowing Water

Nam-myoho-renge-kyo is the foundation of our faith. Mentor and disciple chant with a shared commitment for the realization of kosen-rufu; fellow members, too, chant with unity of purpose, or the spirit of "many in body, one in mind." Chanting this way is the starting point for new progress. It gives fresh impetus to our efforts. It also leads to a wide unfolding of benefit.

Nam-myoho-renge-kyo chanted with the resonance, dynamism, and forward momentum of freely flowing water constitutes a winning rhythm. It's important that we chant at an invigorating pace resembling that of a noble steed galloping across the open plains. Nam-myoho-renge-kyo is the driving force for absolute victory. Chanting with the shared commitment of mentor and disciple and uniting solidly with your fellow members, please always strive with energy and joy to positively develop the young women's division.

You Have Already Won!

There is no way that all of you, who chant Nam-myoho-renge-kyo to the Gohonzon and earnestly strive for kosen-rufu, will fail to become happy. You will not only enjoy happiness in this lifetime but eternally throughout the three existences of past, present, and future.

Real life, however, is filled with an unending series of problems, including such things as financial troubles, sickness, and family disharmony. At such times, your circumstances may seem unfortunate, but if you keep chanting Nam-myoho-renge-kyo throughout, you will definitely transform all that is negative into something positive in accord with the Buddhist principle of "changing poison into medicine." You can ride out every difficulty, turning it into an opportunity for growth. In this sense, on a fundamental level, it can be said that you have already won.

Your life could be likened to a play. You may be performing the role of someone suffering right now, but the play is certain to have a happy and triumphant ending. There is no way that it could conclude in misery. You will enjoy happiness in lifetime after lifetime. You will win eternally, so you have nothing to worry about.

Encouraging a female disciple [the lay nun Toki] who

was challenging various hardships, Nichiren Daishonin writes:

> There is nothing to lament when we consider that we will surely become Buddhas. Even if one were to become an emperor's consort, of what use would it be? Even if one were to be reborn in heaven, what end would it serve? (WND-I, 657)

This disciple had been devotedly caring for her ailing, elderly mother-in-law while struggling with her own illness. Nichiren warmly reassures her that since she is steadfastly deepening her faith in the Lotus Sutra, she will definitely become happy and, therefore, has no reason to lament. He is effectively saying that being born into even the most enviable circumstances cannot possibly compare to the joy of encountering the great teaching of the Mystic Law. He further states:

> Instead, you will follow the way of the dragon king's daughter [the epitome of the enlightenment of women in the Lotus Sutra] and rank with the nun Mahaprajapati [the foremost of Shakyamuni's female disciples]. How wonderful! How wonderful! Please chant Nam-myoho-renge-kyo, Nam-myoho-renge-kyo. (WND-I, 657)

The Joy of Challenge

Having thoroughly studied all the Buddhist sutras, Nichiren clearly articulated an infinitely profound teaching that had never been expounded by any of the non-Buddhist philosophical traditions of India or China or revealed in the Buddhist sutras preached prior to the Lotus Sutra. In other words, he declared for the first time that Nam-myoho-renge-kyo is the ultimate teaching for lasting peace and happiness, and he left this teaching behind for the sake of future generations.

We of the SGI today who embrace the Mystic Law are the most fortunate of all the 6.8 billion people on this planet. Just because someone enjoys favorable circumstances doesn't necessarily mean he or she is happy. One cannot be said to be happy if he or she feels empty inside.

Unsurpassed happiness is found in dedicating one's life to the Mystic Law, the supreme teaching of Buddhism. Happiness isn't the absence of problems or worries. Even Nichiren Daishonin, the Buddha of the Latter Day, encountered great hardships—he faced slander and abuse, incurred intense hatred and jealousy, and battled fierce onslaughts by the three powerful enemies.[1] And he deliberately showed these struggles to his followers as examples for their own Buddhist practice.

True joy can be found in the midst of challenges. Problems can help us grow. Strong opponents can make us stronger. It is just as Nichiren says when he writes, "It is not one's allies but one's powerful enemies who assist one's progress" (WND-I, 770).

As practitioners of Nichiren Buddhism, we not only deal with our own problems and worries but concern ourselves with the welfare of others and the development of kosen-rufu. All of these different problems and concerns motivate us to chant Nam-myoho-renge-kyo. We can also turn them into an impetus for taking the best course of action for our happiness. Faith gives us the strength to tap the life force needed to do so. The Mystic Law is the ultimate key to realize a life of eternity, happiness, true self, and purity.[2]

Five Eternal Guidelines for the Young Women's Division

To commemorate today, my first visit to the Soka Young Women's Center, I'd like to present three poems I have composed especially for you:

Young women's division members
have a profound mission
for kosen-rufu,
hearts shining
as champions of happiness.

Your beautiful gaze
looking far into the distance
is met by the heavenly deities
who praise you
as noble women of victory.

My beloved
young women's division members,
may you advance high-spiritedly
on the path to peace—
Kayo-kai unrivaled in the world!

I'd also like to thank the women's division leaders here today for joining us in spite of their busy schedules. You've all been striving tirelessly for kosen-rufu since your days in the young women's division. I was deeply moved when I saw the inscription on the large plaque in the center's lobby. It contains the lyrics to the young women's division song "Cherry Blossoms of Youth," which we sang together many times (see Section V, p. 125).

The women's division is moving forward vigorously, putting into practice the five guidelines for absolute victory that I presented to them in March this year (2009):

1. Everything begins with prayer.

2. Advancing harmoniously with our families.

3. Fostering young successors.

4. Cherishing our communities and societies.

5. Joyfully sharing our experiences in faith.

Today, I'd like to present five eternal guidelines for the young women's division:

1. Be cheerful suns of happiness.

2. Study the world's foremost life philosophy.

3. Live your youth undefeated by anything.

4. Engage in dialogue to foster friendship and humanistic ideals.

5. Open the gateway to the eternal victory of mentor and disciple.

Please take these five guidelines to heart as you live out your noble youth dedicated to the Mystic Law, filled with great pride and infinite hope.

1. Be Cheerful Suns of Happiness

The first guideline is "Be cheerful suns of happiness." In a letter to Nichigen-nyo, the wife of Shijo Kingo, the Daishonin writes:

> Can anything exceed the sun and moon in brightness? Can anything surpass the lotus flower in purity? The Lotus Sutra is the sun and moon and the lotus flower [in that it is the unsurpassed teaching]. Therefore it is called the Lotus Sutra of the Wonderful Law. Nichiren, too, is like the sun and moon and the lotus flower. (WND-I, 186)

The name *Nichiren* means "sun lotus." Nothing is brighter than the sun, which dispels the darkness.

Nothing is purer than the lotus, which blooms unsullied by the muddy water in which it grows.

The entity of the Law, Myoho-renge-kyo, and the entity of the Person, Nichiren Daishonin, are fully endowed with the functions symbolized by the sun and the lotus. In other words, they are endowed with the power to illuminate the fundamental darkness inherent in life and bring forth the enlightened dharma nature,[3] and the power to purify earthly desires or deluded impulses and transform them into enlightenment.

All of you, the members of the young women's division, have embraced this great teaching of Nam-myoho-renge-kyo at a young age. As such, your lives will shine like the brightest suns and bloom like the purest lotus flowers. That is the purpose of practicing Nichiren Buddhism while in your youth.

The name *Kayo-kai* (Flower-Sun Group) itself has profound meaning from the standpoint of Buddhism. It embodies the fervent prayer that Mr. Toda and my wife and I have shared—the wish that every single member of the young women's division becomes happy.

Create Hope and Joy Yourself

In a letter to another female disciple, the Daishonin likens the great power of the Mystic Law to "a lantern lighting up a place that has been dark for a hundred, a thousand, or ten thousand years" (WND-I, 923). Even the deepest gloom can be illuminated by the light of a lantern. The sun similarly functions to dispel all darkness.

The Daishonin also writes, "When the sun rises in the eastern sky, the light of all the stars fades completely" (WND-I, 959). Even the brightest star pales in the sun's light. Every one of you young women is a sun of happiness, so there is no need for you to lament over your circumstances or to be envious of others. Just chant Nam-myoho-renge-kyo vibrantly and cheerfully bring your life to shine in your own unique way, brimming with courage and self-confidence.

Mahatma Gandhi, the renowned Indian champion of nonviolence, says, "The real ornament of woman is her character, her purity."[4] He also remarked that the more experience he gained in life, the more he realized that human beings themselves are the cause of their own happiness and misery.[5]

Hope and joy aren't things you wait for someone else to give you. Create hope and joy yourself and spread them to others. Youth who choose to live this way are strong. In the same vein, please take the initiative to show appreciation to your hardworking parents and to encourage friends who may be struggling with various problems.

In his treatise "The Object of Devotion for Observing the Mind," the Daishonin writes: "When the skies are clear, the ground is illuminated. Similarly, when one knows the Lotus Sutra, one understands the meaning of all worldly affairs" (WND-1, 376). By applying the Buddhist principle of "substituting faith for wisdom,"[6] all of you who possess such deep faith in the Mystic Law can manifest the lofty life-state of Buddhahood. You can dynamically exercise the wisdom to create value amid the realities of society. And while cheerfully brightening the lives of those around you in the place where you are right now—be it at home, in the workplace, or in your community—you can continue to show wonderful actual proof of faith in terms of gaining trust and achieving success.

There are myriad problems and circumstances that people face, but all of them can definitely be overcome. Mr. Toda often used to say: "Soka Gakkai activities are the shortcut, the direct route to happiness." He spoke widely on the subject of happiness based on faith in Nichiren Buddhism. Allow me to share a few of his words:

> Faith means having the most powerful conviction ourselves. When we chant Nam-myoho-renge-kyo with the firm belief that the heavenly deities will definitely protect us because we are entities of the Mystic Law, then that is precisely what will happen.

> The Gohonzon exists within each of us. . . . When we bring forth the noble Buddha within, we will no longer be unhappy. The power of the Daishonin, the power of the Gohonzon, will fill our being.

> If you practice Nichiren Buddhism, you cannot fail to become happy. Be a person of lofty dignity inside. Proudly live as an honorable member of the Soka Gakkai.

Accumulating Immeasurable Benefit

Mr. Toda continually stressed to the members of the women's and young women's divisions the importance of living their lives based on faith. He once said:

> Believe in the Gohonzon. Believe in the Soka Gakkai. After all, don't we find these words on the left side of the Gohonzon, "Those who make offerings [to the votary of the Lotus Sutra in the Latter Day] will enjoy good fortune surpassing the ten honorable titles"? When you strive your hardest, you accumulate immeasurable benefit. The Gohonzon guarantees this.

The "ten honorable titles" are ten praiseworthy epithets of the Buddha. Through your efforts, all of you can accrue greater benefit than that which derives from making offerings to the Buddha who embodies the virtues of the ten honorable titles.[7]

Mr. Toda also said: "One person's faith, the steadfast commitment to continue chanting to the Gohonzon, is what matters most. The faith of that one person will enable everyone connected to him or her to become happy in the end," and "Just have strong faith, live your lives to the fullest, and become as happy as you possibly can."

Enjoy Your Youth

In life, there are rainy days, cloudy days, and stormy days. No matter what happens, however, it is important that you continue shining brightly as suns of happiness. You can illuminate the lives of everyone around you, now and in the future, with the brilliant light of hope, courage, and victory. I hope you will forge such a state of life while you are still members of the young women's division.

All of you are young, and that's a wonderful thing in itself. The American poet Henry Wadsworth Longfellow, who taught at Harvard University for a time, called on young women to enjoy their youth.[8] I wish the same for each of you.

The Daishonin also writes, "You will grow younger, and your good fortune will accumulate" (WND-1, 464). True to this statement, women who uphold the Mystic

Law can adorn their lives with victory, brimming with youthful vitality and boundless good fortune all of their days. Your seniors in the women's division, including those who are lifetime members of the Seishun-kai (Spring of Youth Group, a young women's group formed in 1975), are all shining testaments to this.

Please live your life vibrantly on the great path of kosen-rufu, true to your vow as a member of the Kayo-kai.

2. Study the World's Foremost Life Philosophy

The second eternal guideline for the young women's division is "Study the world's foremost life philosophy." Nichiren Daishonin clearly states, "If the Law [teaching] that one embraces is supreme, then the person who embraces it must accordingly be foremost among all others" (WND-I, 61). What makes a person truly great? Not wealth, fame, or physical beauty. There are many cases where people enjoy fame for a time but end up leading unhappy lives. True greatness is determined by the teachings we embrace, the philosophy we study, and the extent to which we put these into practice in our daily lives.

All of you who uphold the world's foremost life philosophy of Nichiren Buddhism are leading the most noble and fulfilling youths, the most triumphant, meaningful lives.

You Are the Most Precious Treasure

The French author George Sand was a champion in the struggle of ideas who inspired ordinary people to stand up for social reform. The protagonist in Sand's novel *Consuelo* remarks: "The more I see of [those of noble birth], the more does their lot inspire me with compassion. . . . They are greedy of show and dominion. That is their folly and their misery."[9] This is the keen observation of an insightful writer. Nothing is more pitiful than those who are consumed by arrogance and conceit, and who have been overtaken by the devilish nature of power. You, the members of the young women's division who are striving for the happiness of your friends, the welfare of society, and the realization of a lofty ideal, are far greater and happier than such individuals.

Perhaps it is natural for people to be drawn to bright lights and glamour. It is often thought that fame somehow makes a person special, and those with high social status are often regarded as great. But that is a shallow, deluded way of thinking.

Each of you is the most precious treasure of all. Happiness does not exist outside of you. There is nothing more wonderful than you are. This is what Buddhism teaches. A genuine, meaningful philosophy enables us to bring the most precious treasure that is our life to shine brilliantly.

People tend to compare themselves to others. Of course, it is important to try to learn from others' good traits. But it's petty to envy what appears to be their happiness and good fortune. Nothing comes of that. Those who focus on polishing themselves and living with a sense of purpose are the victors in life. Please engrave this point deeply in your heart.

The Way to the Equality, Dignity, and Happiness of All

The Lotus Sutra embodies a life philosophy that can transform human history. It's a teaching of the enlightenment of women, in particular, and opens the way for the equality, dignity, and happiness of all humanity. Nichiren writes: "The enlightenment of women is expounded as a model [for the enlightenment of all living beings]" (WND-I, 930), and "Among the teachings of the Lotus Sutra, that of women attaining Buddhahood is first" (WND-I, 930).

Through the earnest prayers and unflagging efforts of your noble predecessors in the young women's and women's divisions, we are now ushering in an age of women. A stage for your activities extends throughout the world.

In the Daishonin's treatise "The True Aspect of All Phenomena," we find this important passage:

> Exert yourself in the two ways of practice and study. Without practice and study, there can be no Buddhism. You must not only persevere yourself; you must also teach others. Both practice and study arise from faith. Teach others to the best of your ability, even if it is only a single sentence or phrase. (WND-I, 386)

I hope you will all experience for yourselves and demonstrate to others just how sublime is a youth spent exerting oneself in the two ways of practice and study, as the Daishonin urges.

Nichiren also writes:

> Others read the Lotus Sutra with their mouths alone, in word alone, but they do not read it with their hearts. And even if they read it with their hearts, they do not read it with their actions. It is reading the sutra with both one's body and mind [as you have by encountering this hardship] that is truly praiseworthy! (WND-I, 204)

Encountering life-threatening persecution as a result of speaking out to protect the correct teaching in exact accord with Nichiren's spirit and battling dauntlessly against all manner of obstacles—this is the proud history of our Soka movement based on the mentor-disciple relationship. I hope that you, our young women's division members, will continue along this honorable path.

The Joy of Discovering Life's Depth

"The members of the young women's division must make study their foundation!" This is a guiding principle articulated by my mentor, second Soka Gakkai president

Josei Toda. Nichiren Buddhism is the ultimate philosophy of happiness and peace. Through its wisdom, we can transform our lives on a fundamental level, bring people together, and change the destiny of the world.

Mr. Toda observed, "No matter how much humanity may come to understand the physical world, it won't lead to inner happiness." He also said: "The Daishonin sought to find a way to enable all people to attain happiness. When we earnestly study and put into practice the life philosophy of Nichiren Buddhism, it will shine as the ultimate teaching for becoming absolutely happy."

Speaking of the importance of philosophy, Mr. Toda said:

Why do we need philosophy? Why do our lives need the Daishonin's Buddhism? If it were enough to just do as we pleased, there'd be no need to go to school and study or have religious faith. But if we follow that course, we'll only come to regret it later. On the other hand, what incredible joy there is to be found in studying philosophy, studying Buddhism, and discovering the depth of life, and, based on that, seeking and attaining true and lasting happiness with an open heart and profound emotion. What an immeasurable delight it is to know the deeply wondrous nature of life and experience our own being brimming with limitless joy!

He also said:

With the Gohonzon as our foundation, we of the Soka Gakkai are advancing toward the lofty goal of kosen-rufu. And we carry out our practice basing ourselves on the study of the Daishonin's Buddhism, the world's greatest life philosophy, the essence of the entirety of Shakyamuni's teachings.

The karmic ties we share as fellow members working together for kosen-rufu with the Soka Gakkai are profound indeed.

Mr. Toda made the following remarks to the young women's division:

Closely examining human existence, Buddhism solidly brings together the four viewpoints of self, life, society, and the universe.

❖

Read the Daishonin's writings more intently.
Everything you need is written there.

If you make the Daishonin's writings your
foundation, you will never be swayed by any
problems you may encounter.

If you base yourself on the supreme value of the
Mystic Law, you'll always know how to proceed.

If we look at things from the perspective of faith, the
way forward will become clear to us. Do not be deceived
by empty appearances or hypocrisy.

The members of the young women's division study
department have given their all to create a fine record
of achievement in promoting Buddhist study. Establishing a firm pillar of Buddhist study in the hearts of young
people who are often swayed by their environment is of
immense importance.

I'd like to share a few more confident words that
Mr. Toda spoke to our precious young women's division

members: "Start by deciding what you will do and how you will challenge yourself. That is philosophy." He also said: "Only we of the Soka Gakkai are actually practicing the philosophy of Nam-myoho-renge-kyo. I want all of you, our young women's division members, to make this philosophy an integral part of your lives and carry out kosen-rufu. I'm counting on you!"

A Youth Spent Learning

The French philosopher Alain (the pseudonym of philosopher and essayist Emile Chartier) writes in his work *On Happiness:* "They say that happiness always eludes us. That is true for happiness that we have handed to us, for there is no such happiness. But the happiness we make for ourselves is not illusory. It is a learning process, and one never stops learning."[10] A youth spent learning sets one on a trajectory to happiness.

Some of the young women here today are also student division leaders. I hope the student division members will apply themselves to their studies with enthusiasm and cultivate outstanding character and ability.

Have Unshakable Faith

The Russian author Leo Tolstoy summarized what he learned from the teachings of the Buddha he read, "If people speak and act based on positive ideals, joy will follow them as a shadow follows a body."[11]

A young women's division member who is a Soka school graduate and has a doctorate in Russian literature translated some of Tolstoy's diary entries written nearly a century ago and sent them to me. One of them reads, "To the degree that you treasure the present moment, you are able to live an eternal and unshakable life."[12] How true this is.

I call on all of you to accumulate eternal good fortune and forge unshakable faith while you are in the young women's division. My wife also established a solid foundation of faith when she was a young women's division member. She dedicated herself tirelessly to kosen-rufu, sharing the Daishonin's teachings with others, encouraging her fellow members, and fostering capable people. She exerted herself wholeheartedly to realize Mr. Toda's vision, a commitment that remains unchanged to this day. To reply to our mentor, to work selflessly for kosen-rufu and the happiness of our members—this is the true Soka Gakkai spirit.

3. *Live Your Youth Undefeated by Anything*

The third eternal guideline for the young women's division is "Live your youth undefeated by anything." Nichiren writes: "A woman who embraces this sutra [the Lotus Sutra] not only excels all other women, but also surpasses all men" (WND-I, 464). How incredibly noble you are!

Throughout his writings, the Daishonin repeatedly encourages his female disciples. For example, he declares, "A woman who embraces the lion king of the Lotus Sutra never fears any of the beasts of hell or of the realms of hungry spirits and animals" (WND-I, 949). The fact that you uphold the Mystic Law means that you will never be defeated by anything.

The Daishonin also writes: "Although the sun and moon should fall to the ground and Mount Sumeru[13] crumble, there can be no doubt that this woman [of sincere faith] will attain Buddhahood" (WND-2, 752); and "Whatever trouble occurs, regard it as no more than a dream, and think only of the Lotus Sutra" (WND-I, 502). It's foolish to let oneself be swayed by life's uncertainties, feeling joy one minute, despair the next. Resolve to dedicate your life to kosen-rufu no matter what, and spend your youth confidently committed to your mission. Never forget that beautiful flowers of happiness bloom forth where there are solid roots of perseverance and effort.

Make Safety and Health Top Priorities

My mentor, second Soka Gakkai president Josei Toda, once remarked: "If we uphold the Gohonzon and exert ourselves assiduously in faith, practice, and study, we will not forever remain deluded, unenlightened people at the mercy of various sufferings." He also said: "When we look back later, even the most painful experiences eventually fade and vanish like a dream. That's why we must remember to be patient and to persevere, taking a long-term perspective and biding our time." He also said: "Cultivate perseverance. Doesn't the Daishonin urge us to 'don the armor of endurance' (see WND-1, 392)? I would like you to regard perseverance as the essence of true Buddhist practice."

Mr. Toda often said that in our youth, we should focus less on winning and more on not being defeated. My wife followed his guidance to the letter, living an undefeated youth and an undefeated life. She has truly won. I hope you will do the same.

In these troubled times, please take care not to come into harm's way. Please be guided by wisdom and good sense in your daily affairs, making safety and health your top priorities and especially ensuring that Buddhist activities don't go on too late at night so that you can go home at a reasonable hour.

Build a Strong, Unshakable State of Life

Courage is vital. Rosa Luxemburg, the Polish-German revolutionary, called on her comrades: "Fear nothing!"[14] and "Be courageous. Have courage!"[15]

Incidentally, at a summer training course held in 1969, a group of student division members performed a musical tribute to this heroic activist. Forty years have flown by since then, and I am very happy that all of those young women are today striving with unchanged enthusiasm as leaders in the women's division.

The American poet Emily Dickinson writes:

> *On a columnar self*
> *How ample to rely;*

In tumult or extremity
How good the certainty.[16]

Faith in Nichiren Buddhism enables us to build a strong, unshakable state of life that is never swayed by anything, as do Buddhist activities, especially those in our youth.

The great Renaissance artist and inventor Leonardo da Vinci writes, "Nothing flows faster than the years."[17] Speaking of Leonardo da Vinci, I fondly recall delivering an address (in June 1994) titled "Leonardo's Universal Vision and the Parliament of Humanity: Thoughts on the Future of the United Nations" at the University of Bologna, one of the world's oldest universities. As da Vinci pointed out, the years pass by quickly. Our youth only comes but once. All of you, the members of the young women's division, are now in the midst of the wonderful time of youth. I therefore hope you will strive your hardest and do your best to spread our noble Soka movement.

"I'll Take Care of It!"

To be young is to possess vast potential. In my youth, I struggled and fought with all my might. After World

War II, Mr. Toda's businesses collapsed and he was left shouldering enormous debts. Some who worked for Mr. Toda cursed and abandoned him. He eventually decided to step down as the Soka Gakkai's general director [in order to shield the organization from his business problems]. At that challenging time, however, I vowed to continue working for Mr. Toda and support him every way possible. I was a young man in my twenties, and I did my utmost to assist my mentor.

Gradually, his business situation turned around, and Mr. Toda was inaugurated as the second president of the Soka Gakkai (in May 1951). But then propagation efforts stagnated, and Mr. Toda lamented that, at this rate, it would take fifty thousand years to achieve kosen-rufu. Once again I stood up and declared, "I'll take care of it!" Spearheading the propagation campaign in Tokyo's Kamata Chapter (in February 1952), I broke through the stalemate and opened the way to the realization of Mr. Toda's cherished lifetime goal of 750,000 Soka Gakkai member-households. I helped set a new record of dynamic growth in propagation and created the momentum for the fresh development of our movement.

Be People Who Are Indispensable

Right after World War II, I found a job at a small printing company called Shobundo. The company owner was very happy with my work and hoped I'd remain with them long term. Unfortunately, because of my poor health, after only a short time there, I had to quit and take another job closer to home at the Kamata Manufacturers Association. A few years later, I decided to leave that job when I was given the opportunity to work at Mr. Toda's company. My boss and co-workers were sad to see me go, and they threw me a heartfelt farewell party.

Being someone who is indispensable and trusted at work is the hallmark of a genuine youth division member. I hope our Soka youth will be the kind of people who are considered crucial assets for the positive development of their workplaces. Moreover, if you strive earnestly in faith and do your best at work each day, you will absolutely become such a person.

No Regrets

All of you are sincerely chanting Nam-myoho-renge-kyo and working for the happiness of others. You are striving hard in Soka Gakkai activities. Nothing is nobler than this. Without a doubt, the Daishonin is praising and applauding your efforts. You are sure to attain clear and wonderful benefits. It doesn't matter whether others are aware of your efforts or not. When you dedicate your life to kosen-rufu, you will have no regrets. All of your struggles will have meaning and become causes for your victory. Please continue to fight alongside me as proud Soka Gakkai members!

Keep Pressing Forward

The noted American cultural anthropologist Dr. Mary Catherine Bateson writes, "No one can expect, of course, to go through life without meeting discouragement and criticism, but every failure [experienced by a woman] is more costly if it is accompanied by the implied message from outside, and the hidden belief within, that little more could have been expected."[18] I hope all of our young women's division members will live their lives unafraid of failure. Remain encouraged, no matter what happens, and keep pressing forward. The important thing is that you win in the end.

I have heard, incidentally, that the ideas I presented in my second address at Harvard (in September 1993) —namely, that joy can be savored in both life and death—struck a deep chord with Dr. Bateson.[19]

Remain Young at Heart

A character in one of the novels written by Danish author and storyteller Hans Christian Andersen says: "There will come better days! Happy days! [You are] young, and youth brings health for the soul and body!"[20] To remain undefeated by troubles and triumph over them are the challenge and inherent strength of youth. May all of you be healthy and optimistic in your youth.

Of course, you mustn't lose your vitality even when you grow older. Those who uphold the Mystic Law can remain youthful throughout their lives. Please forever continue to have the hearts of young women's division members, just as your dynamic seniors in the women's division have.

Some of you may be worrying about marriage. I hope you won't hesitate to discuss your specific concerns with your parents, your seniors in the women's division, or someone else you can trust. Moreover, it is crucial above all to chant earnestly to the Gohonzon. There's no need to be anxious or in a hurry. Getting married at a young age doesn't necessarily guarantee happiness. Just chant so that you'll meet a wonderful person and have a marriage that is ideal for you. I'd like you to polish your life through faith and shine in your own unique way.

Hans Christian Andersen also writes:

> *Laughter lightens every sadness.*
> *Trust me, the people we praise*
> *Have usually attained their happiness through*
>   *laughter.*
>
> . . .
>
> *Laughter can even win over our enemies.*[21]

My wife, who received training as Mr. Toda's disciple from her days in the young women's division, always has a smile, no matter how difficult the situation. I hope that all of you, my young friends, will also joyfully move ahead no matter what happens and that you will chant Nam-myoho-renge-kyo wholeheartedly and bring forth a powerful life force. I assert that as long as the joy of faith shines from the smiling faces of young women's division members, the Soka Gakkai will be strong and continue growing.

4. Engage in Dialogue to Foster Friendship and Humanistic Ideals

One person's sincerity can be truly inspiring. One person's faith can have a tremendous impact on others.

In a letter addressed to a follower known as the lady of Sajiki, Nichiren Daishonin describes the profound significance of making an offering to the Lotus Sutra: "To illustrate, if a spark as small as a bean is set to a single blade of grass in a spring field of a thousand square [miles] thick with grass, it becomes in an instant an immeasurable, boundless blaze. Such is also the case with [your offering of a single robe]" (WND-1, 533). This is a vivid metaphor. The Daishonin also teaches that the benefit a person gains from making an offering to the Law will extend to family and loved ones, including parents and grandparents and indeed the lives of everyone to whom that person is connected (see WND-1, 533).

Everything starts with a single action. A single word of encouragement can inspire courage. Embodying these great principles, your seniors in the women's division have expanded the stage of kosen-rufu. On June 10 (2009), our admirable women's division will celebrate its fifty-eighth anniversary. Congratulations!

We Make Our Own History

Eleanor Roosevelt, in addition to being a social activist and former American first lady, is well known as having played a major role in the drafting of the Universal Declaration of Human Rights. In her later years, she writes, "It is my conviction that there is almost no arena of life which we cannot transform according to our own desires if we want something badly enough, if we have faith in it, and if we work for it with all our hearts."[22] These words also echo the resolve of the women of Soka.

We uphold the supreme teaching of the Mystic Law and are pursuing the great path of kosen-rufu. Faith in Nichiren Buddhism gives us the power to positively transform even seemingly insurmountable obstacles.

Mrs. Roosevelt also writes: "One thing I believe profoundly: We make our own history. The course of history is directed by the choices we make and our choices grow out of the ideas, the beliefs, the values, the dreams of the people."[23] The grass-roots movement of the SGI is creating a new history, initiating a shift from war to peace, from conflict to harmonious coexistence, from resignation to hope. Together, let's dedicate our lives to the monumental dream of kosen-rufu!

Wholeheartedly Engage In Dialogue

The fourth new guideline for the young women's division is "Engage in dialogue to foster friendship and humanistic ideals." Dialogue is extremely important in Nichiren Buddhism.

The Daishonin writes, "This saha world is a land in which one gains the way through the faculty of hearing" (WND-2, 87). Teaching another person about the Mystic Law and enabling him or her to form a connection with Buddhism is the supremely noble work of Buddhas. The dialogues you are carrying out to share the Daishonin's teachings with others are directly linked to the expansion of happiness and humanism.

The Daishonin states: "[Having] heard the Lotus Sutra, which leads to Buddhahood, with this as the seed, one will invariably become a Buddha" (WND-1, 882); and "One should by all means persist in preaching the Lotus Sutra and causing [others] to hear it" (WND-1, 882). We mustn't spare our voices in sharing the unsurpassed principles of Nichiren Buddhism with as many people as possible. Through such efforts, we help connect others to Buddhism, the path to eternal happiness. At the same time, we engrave experiences of everlasting good fortune in our lives. The Daishonin declares, "Single-mindedly chant Nam-myoho-renge-kyo and urge others to do the same; that will remain as the only memory of your present life in this human world" (WND-1, 64).

Speak With Conviction

We must be confident and unhesitant in sharing the greatness of Nichiren Buddhism with others. As the Daishonin writes, "You must act and speak without the least servility" (WND-1, 824). Having the strength to plainly state things as they are is the *shakubuku* spirit, the Soka Gakkai spirit, and the spirit of kosen-rufu. Our organization is what it is today because our members have this proud strength.

Discussing the essence of dialogue, Mr. Toda said, "Sincerely sharing the truth with others and expressing what's in our heart—these are the principles that gave birth to the Soka Gakkai and are the driving force of its development." He also remarked: "Important is humanistic dialogue that fosters genuine heart-to-heart communication, friendship, and understanding of different cultures."

In addition, he taught me: "Just launching into an abstract discussion of difficult Buddhist principles doesn't necessarily contribute to people's understanding of Buddhism. Sometimes it's better to take a more creative and flexible approach and share the humanistic ideals of the Daishonin's teaching through such subjects as literature, music, and art."

Cherishing my mentor's instructions, I have striven to engage in dialogue that transcends all barriers. Together with my wife, I have opened paths of dialogue and built bridges of friendship around the globe. This is a precious legacy that I bequeath to all of you. As philosophers of Soka, please engage in dialogue freely, joyfully, to your heart's content.

Lead Sincere Lives Based on Buddhism

Now I'd like to share some thoughts from writers around the world. The German author Johann Wolfgang von Goethe believed that honesty is the most admirable quality of all.[24] The heavenly deities—the positive forces of the universe—will always protect people of sincerity and integrity who base their lives on Buddhism.

The American writer Eleanor H. Porter writes, "The bigger [the person], the more simple and unassuming [he or she is]."[25] Leaders exist to wholeheartedly serve the members, not to act self-important. I hope you will also remember this point.

The American philosopher and essayist Ralph Waldo Emerson writes, "I find this law of *one to one* [vital] for conversation, which is the practice and consummation of friendship."[26] A life that is committed to building bonds of friendship through one-on-one dialogue is truly noble. Moreover, to share lofty ideals and principles through dialogue is our pride as global citizens.

The Daishonin writes, "You should always talk with each other to free yourselves from the sufferings of birth and death and attain the pure land of Eagle Peak, where you will nod to each other and speak in one mind" (WND-I, 909). The Mystic Law enables us to achieve, together with our fellow members, a state of life forever imbued with eternity, happiness, true self, and purity.

The American writer and social activist Helen Keller, who was both blind and deaf, writes, "Ideas are mightier than fire and sword. Noiselessly they propagate themselves from land to land, and mankind goes out and reaps the rich harvest."[27] All of you are sincerely reaching out to others in dialogue each day. These steady, grassroots efforts will accumulate and eventually result in the great blossoming of kosen-rufu worldwide.

In one of his poems, Goethe writes of encountering a little flower on the side of the road. Charmed by its beauty, he tries to pick it, but the flower speaks to him:

I have roots,
hidden from view.

I am grounded
in deep soil.
That's why we flowers
grow so beautifully.[28]

Only through continuous efforts that are often unknown to others and by establishing deep and solid roots in the earth of the Mystic Law can you bring the precious flower of your own unique mission to bloom. That flower will spread innumerable seeds of hope throughout the world and into the future.

5. Open the Gateway to the Eternal Victory of Mentor and Disciple

The fifth eternal guideline for the young women's division is "Open the gateway to the eternal victory of mentor and disciple." A well-known passage from the writings of Nichiren Daishonin states that women open the gateway (see WND-2, 884). One young woman can open the gateway to great happiness and prosperity for many others. In this phrase *open the gateway,* I cannot help but sense the Daishonin's profound aspirations for women.

In the Lotus Sutra, the dragon king's daughter, amid an atmosphere of prejudice and discrimination against women, overturns the traditionally accepted values of the day with her enlightenment. Because she attains the state of Buddhahood as she is, she demonstrates that all living beings can do the same. According to the Lotus Sutra, when this event happens, "hearts [are] filled with great joy" (LSOC, 228) and everyone in the *saha* world pays homage to the dragon king's daughter.

I presented a calligraphy of this same phrase, "hearts filled with great joy," to the young women's division to commemorate the completion of this Soka Young Women's Center with my prayers for the success of all the young women who are opening the gateway of hope of kosen-rufu.

Fulfilling the Vow of One's Youth

The dragon king's daughter says to her teacher Shakyamuni:

[You] the Buddha alone can bear witness to this
[my attaining enlightenment].

I unfold the doctrines of the great vehicle [the
Lotus Sutra] to rescue living beings from suffering. (LSOC, 227)

Deeply confident that her teacher understands her completely, she pledges to strive her hardest together with
him without begrudging her life.

Making a vow to work alongside our mentor to further kosen-rufu and do our best to encourage others has
nothing to do with our position, title, or physical distance from our mentor.

A profound pledge is also infused in the Ikeda Kayo-
kai song, "The Vow of the Ikeda Kayo-kai." As you, the
present members of the Kayo-kai, strive to fulfill the vow
of your youth, you are all enacting a magnificent drama
of the victory of kosen-rufu. Without a doubt, the network you are building will be looked to as a model of
hope by future generations.

Leading Lives of Complete Freedom

Tokiko Tada (nee Minato) is one of your seniors in faith who widely opened the gateway to the victory of mentor and disciple. Born in October 1925, she lost her father before she was five years old. She suffered from a poor constitution, and World War II colored the early years of her youth. Shortly after the war ended, her beloved mother also passed away. She was on the verge of total despair when she encountered Nichiren Buddhism. She became a member of the Soka Gakkai in August 1951 (at age 26).

My wife, at that time a young women's division group leader, enshrined the Gohonzon bestowed on Mrs. Tada. Though my wife was several years younger, she continued to encourage Mrs. Tada as a senior in faith and close friend. Through her Buddhist practice, Mrs. Tada pulled herself up from the depths of misery and poverty and went on to lead a vigorous and meaningful youth. Chosen as one of the members of the original Kayo-kai, she received training directly from second Soka Gakkai president Josei Toda.

The people we meet and the guidance we encounter can have tremendous influence on our lives.

On May 3, 1958, right after Mr. Toda's death, Mrs. Tada was appointed as the national young women's division leader of the Soka Gakkai. Within five years, she helped increase the membership of the young women's division sevenfold, from 55,000 to 400,000. Later, a month after she was appointed the national women's division leader in July 1968, the Soka Gakkai song today known around the world as "Forever Sensei" debuted as a song for the Japanese women's division.

In the 1970s, Mrs. Tada also helped pioneer a new age of women as a member of the House of Representatives (the Lower House of Japan's Diet). After retiring from politics, she returned to the front lines of our movement and strove to repay her debt of gratitude to the Soka Gakkai and her fellow members by fostering numerous successors. Mrs. Tada also met with many well-known international figures.

As she so vividly showed us, those who base themselves on the Mystic Law can truly lead lives of complete freedom, attaining a boundless state of being in sublime communication with the heavenly deities and Buddhas and bodhisattvas throughout the universe. The lives of such people shine with unsurpassed glory and brilliance. I hope you have deep confidence in this.

A Source of Strength

What's the key to leading a life of freedom and joy? The noted American cultural anthropologist Dr. Bateson suggests that one important factor is realizing "that difference [i.e., one's uniqueness] can be a source of strength rather than weakness."[29] This is a very astute observation.

As members of the Soka Gakkai, we are all practicing Nichiren Buddhism, a teaching of infinite hope. This itself is our greatest strength.

Mr. Toda often said, "The Soka Gakkai should be a gathering of people who uphold the mentor-disciple spirit and advance together in a common struggle no matter what happens." Genuine disciples are those who make the mentor's heart their own and share the joys and sufferings of their fellow members. In contrast, those who, driven by self-interest, are envious of the truly admirable and arrogantly look down on their fellow members inevitably come to a miserable end. You have all borne witness to this fact.

The political theorist Hannah Arendt observed that envy is invariably connected to arrogance.[30] I hope each of you, rather than envying others, will be shining examples who inspire admiration and emulation.

Life Is the Most Precious Treasure

Congratulations on the fortieth anniversary of the establishment of the Shirakaba Group, the young women's division nurses group! The members of the Shirakaba-kai, the women's division nurses group, are also working very hard. Your constant care for the health of others, including your fellow members, is infinitely noble.

There is no treasure more precious than life. I have always asserted that our society should highly esteem and honor nurses, who are dedicated to protecting life.

In this age of disregard for life, our Shirakaba nurses, who embrace the life-affirming philosophy of Nichiren Buddhism, are creating a century of life. They are true experts and examples of compassion. My wife and I sincerely hope and pray that the Shirakaba spirit will spread across the globe. Let us work together with the Shirakaba members toward making this century one that respects the dignity of life.

The Highest Respect for Women

Women are making especially noteworthy contributions to our movement for kosen-rufu. And leaders in various fields of society are acknowledging the outstanding efforts of our young women's division members.

Buddhism teaches gender equality. Every woman who upholds the Mystic Law is a supremely noble individual with a unique and precious mission. The men in our organization should sincerely respect and support women with a spirit of profound gratitude and appreciation. If they pay greater attention to doing so, the momentum for kosen-rufu will grow exponentially. In the realm of the Soka Gakkai, women also need to speak out and rebuke male leaders who behave in a domineering or contemptuous manner toward them.

Mr. Toda declared: "Kosen-rufu will be achieved through the power of women. The efforts of women are truly noble." He also said that strengthening and increasing the membership of the young women's division will open the gateway to the eternal victory of kosen-rufu and the eternal development of the Soka Gakkai. I know that Mr. Toda would be overjoyed to see all of you, the wonderful members of today's young women's division.

I cannot help but feel that I have a mystic connection with you, the young women who, in this culminating period of my life, are striving wholeheartedly to fulfill the vow of the Kayo-kai. I wish to fully entrust the future of kosen-rufu to you, my young friends in the young women's division, who are our most valued treasures. My wife and I are watching over you with that prayer in our hearts.

An Inspiration for All

Earlier this year (in March 2009), as a graduate of what I fondly refer to as "Toda University" and as your representative, I received an honorary doctorate from Denmark's University College South. On that occasion, I also received a medal bearing the images of three famous Danish people, including the storyteller and writer Hans Christian Andersen. Andersen declares, "The world is young, / so be young with the young!"[31] In the same spirit as Andersen, I declare with boundless hope and aspirations for you: "Soka is young, / so be young with the Kayo-kai members!" and "The future is bright, / so be bright with the Kayo-kai members!"

To commemorate our meeting today, I would also like to present a framed photograph of the *Dendrobium Kaneko Ikeda* orchid, named by the Singapore Botanic Gardens.

To all Ikeda Kayo-kai members everywhere, I wish to dedicate this poem:

Noble
and elegantly fragrant,
the Kaneko orchid—
may the princesses of the Kayo-kai
joyfully follow her example.

I wish to offer three cheers to the Kayo-kai members in Tokyo, throughout Japan, and around the world. Please bring beautiful flowers of the victory of mentor and disciple into bloom on the stage of your mission. Give my very best regards to your parents and to the members who couldn't be here today.

[*The members then joined in singing the Ikeda Kayo-kai song, "The Vow of the Ikeda Kayo-kai."*]

What a wonderful song! Thank you!

With this song in your heart and remaining ever true to your vow, please advance vibrantly throughout your life. Take care of your health. Work together harmoniously. Create a magnificent record of achievement, one free of any regrets!

Be well! Let's meet again!

(Translated from the June 11, 2009, *Seikyo Shimbun,* the Soka Gakkai's daily newspaper)

Essays

From the series The Light of the Century of Humanity

Young Women, Bright Like the Sun

By Shin'ichi Yamamoto

> *The sun shines*
> *brilliantly*
> *in your beautiful*
> *flowerlike hearts,*
> *filling you with radiance.*

May 3 is upon us once more! It is a time when the heavens and our hearts rejoice. With appreciation for the dedicated efforts of our noble members around the world, I wish to express my warmest congratulations to everyone on Soka Gakkai Day and Soka Gakkai Mother's Day. For Soka mentors and disciples, May 3 is a day of proud triumph and a day when we courageously set out toward fresh victories. Let's advance forever, leading the way with a positive and dynamic spirit!

The bright young women's division members are working energetically for peace, their efforts heralding the arrival of a new age in our Soka movement. Brimming with joy, a solid network of young women—united with their mentor and committed to pioneering the second act of kosen-rufu—has now been firmly established. They form the Ikeda Kayo-kai. While the present members of the group constitute its first "class," a second and a third and countless other "classes" will steadily follow, creating a beautiful, admirable, and mighty stream of capable individuals that will flow on into the eternal future. This group is truly sublime and noble.

A new age has come. A new century has arrived. The soaring peaks of global kosen-rufu are now visible. How wonderful this is. I would like to congratulate you!

To commemorate the establishment of their new group, the young women's division members have presented us with an antique clock they have named the Kayo Clock. The word *kayo* comprises the Chinese characters for *flower* and *sun,* or *sunshine;* it is symbolic of flowers that are bathed in brilliant sunlight and are a boundless source of lofty inspiration for others.

It is my wish that all our young women will play a wonderful melody of happiness and peace during this precious time of their youth, in rhythm with the Kayo

Clock as it marks the passage of time. Watching over the activities and growth of these youthful, beautiful-hearted members together with my wife, I have also steadily begun to write a new page of great development for worldwide kosen-rufu.

Spiritedly forging ahead
as noble heroines
in the struggle of kosen-rufu,
Kayo-kai members will leave
their legacy in the citadel of Soka.

My mentor, second Soka Gakkai president Josei Toda, firmly believed that the realization of kosen-rufu depends upon women. In October 1952, he formed a young women's division group called the Kayo-kai (Flower-Sun Group), the fostering of which he devoted himself to.

In a letter to one of his followers, Nichigen-nyo [the wife of Shijo Kingo], Nichiren Daishonin writes:

Can anything exceed the sun and moon in brightness? Can anything surpass the lotus flower in purity? The Lotus Sutra is the sun and moon

and the lotus flower. Therefore it is called the
Lotus Sutra of the Wonderful Law [Myoho-
renge-kyo]. Nichiren, too, is like the sun and
moon and the lotus flower. (WND-I, 186)

The lives of the young women of Soka who uphold
the Mystic Law and dedicate themselves to kosen-rufu
just as the Daishonin teaches are like the brightest of
suns and the purest of lotus flowers. In other words, their
lives themselves are the epitome of everything for which
the Kayo-kai stands.

> *May each and every*
> *Kayo-kai member,*
> *a sparkling gem of*
> *dedication to the Buddha's decree,*
> *shine throughout the three existences.*

In April 1958, when my mentor passed away, the
young women's division comprised thirty-eight corps. By
May 3, one month later, when a new national young
women's division leader was also appointed, that number had grown to fifty. My wife, incidentally, was a close

friend of the new leader, having encouraged her in faith since the beginning of her practice. This leader was none other than Tokiko Tada (nee Minato).

The first Kayo-kai meeting I attended in my late mentor's place was in October 1958. As I recall, it was a guidance meeting held on the shore of Lake Ashi in Hakone (in Kanagawa Prefecture). At the time, I was the de facto leader of the entire Soka Gakkai, its sole general administrator, bearing full responsibility for kosen-rufu. More than half of those in attendance on that occasion were new members of the group.

The young women's division continued to grow by leaps and bounds. By the time I was inaugurated as the third president of the Soka Gakkai two years later, on May 3, 1960, it had more than doubled to 108 corps.

The ancient Greek poet Pindar sang: "Wonder at the courage and mighty strength of a woman, what a contest she is waging with undaunted [mind], . . . having a heart superior to toil."[32]

The remarkable development of the young women's division astonished all our members and filled them with immeasurable hope.

The dazzling
hearts of young women
united with their mentor.

When capable people come to the fore, a new age opens. Future victory depends on successfully fostering young leaders.

Florence Nightingale, founder of the modern nursing profession, is well known for her emphasis on the importance of training and lifelong learning. In particular, she warned her students not to let their "time of training slip away."[33] Those who receive training in their youth move forward along the path to victory in life.

In July 1960, an outdoor training session of the Kayo-kai was held at Futtsu Beach in Chiba Prefecture. Nearly all the members of the group were new, so this gathering in effect marked the full-fledged start of the second "class" of Kayo-kai members. These gatherings of the Kayo-kai, which I personally attended, continued until 1968.

For a little more than a decade, I, too, received personal training and instruction from my mentor, Mr. Toda, on philosophy and leadership—lessons far more valuable than those found in mountains of books. In the same way, in the decade I spent training the members of the

Kayo-kai, I did my best to fully communicate to them the essence of a life dedicated to kosen-rufu.

The Kayo-kai meeting conducted in Hakone in July 1966 was particularly memorable. I read aloud the short story "Run, Melos!" by Japanese author Osamu Dazai, which the members had studied in advance.

Incidentally, we were honored this year to have a member of Dazai's family attend the exhibition Children and a Culture of Peace, which was organized by the Soka Gakkai Women's Peace Committee in Tokyo.

Based on a poem by the German writer Friedrich von Schiller,[34] "Run, Melos!" is well known in Japan. It tells the story of a cruel and tyrannical king who has lost faith in human goodness and loyalty and is executing many people. The young shepherd Melos rises up against the king in righteous outrage but is apprehended and sentenced to death. He requests as his last wish that he be allowed to return to his village to attend his younger sister's wedding. The king will not let him go without a hostage to remain in his place, and Melos's dear friend Selinuntius volunteers. Melos leaves for his village, promising to return before sunset three days later as the king stipulates.

If Melos keeps his promise, his friend will be freed and Melos will be executed. Will Melos go back by the designated time, or betray his friend to save his own life?

After his sister's wedding, Melos sets out to return to the king, intending to keep his promise and save the life of the friend who trusted him. But his way back is blocked by a raging flood caused by a torrential downpour. He eventually manages to swim through the flood, only to be attacked by bandits. He escapes from them, but as sunset approaches on the third day, Melos starts to waver as he is swamped by exhaustion and the desire to give up trying.

Melos rallies his spirit, however, and, rejecting these cowardly inner whisperings, triumphs over temptation. "Someone waits for me," he thinks. "I must prove worthy of his trust."

"Run, Melos!" he tells himself, spurring himself on until he arrives just in time to save his friend from execution. By remaining true to his promise and coming back to save Selinuntius, Melos demonstrates to the king that loyalty does exist. He thus succeeds in restoring the latter's faith in human beings. [As a result, the king spares both Melos and his friend.]³⁵

Before I began reading at the meeting, I said to the participants with deep emotion: "I would like to dedicate this story to all of you, in tribute to the Kayo-kai. The spirit it depicts mirrors my own history and my future course, as well as my personal determination. I hope that you will all struggle fearlessly, too, in your personal battles!"

Looking back, when President Toda's businesses were in crisis and the very survival of the Soka Gakkai was threatened, I ran like Melos to protect my mentor. During the Osaka campaign of 1956[36] as well, I fought and won with unswerving determination, as if I were Melos myself. After my mentor's death, I overcame every fierce storm of adversity and ran tirelessly to demonstrate the truth and victory of the Soka Gakkai to the entire world. With the indefatigable spirit of Melos, I dedicated myself to fulfilling the pledge I made to my mentor as his disciple.

As Osamu Dazai proclaims, "Do the right thing with a smile!"[37]

❖

Young Women, Blaze a Golden Path
Rise above
the sad and foolish self-defeated ones
who have cast away their faith,
and proceed to the jeweled summit
that awaits the Kayo-kai.

There have been many people throughout the history of our movement who betrayed their mentors to whom they were greatly indebted, caused suffering to their fellow members, and tried to harm the Soka Gakkai. All of you have seen the wretched and hellish state of life into which these unfortunate individuals have subsequently fallen. No matter what clever arguments they might present to justify their actions, they have engineered their downfall through their own self-betrayal.

I'll never forget the words the youthful Mongolian president Nambaryn Enkhbayar shared with me during our meeting (in February 2007). They were some lines from a Mongolian folk song: "We speak of hell, but where does hell come from? / Breaking a vow you have made—that is hell."[38]

In the course of life, we are bound to meet with various hardships and occasional, unexpected storms of destiny. It is also certain, in the light of the Lotus Sutra and the Daishonin's writings, that the Soka Gakkai—an organization of votaries of the Lotus Sutra—will be targeted for attack by the three powerful enemies[39] of Buddhism. And it is also only natural that individuals who have abandoned and betrayed their faith out of envy or ingratitude will plot against us. Each such challenge presents what the Daishonin calls a "crucial moment" (WND-1, 283).[40] What counts at that time is whether one remains true to one's vow for kosen-rufu—as the Daishonin declares, "This is my vow, and I will never forsake it!" (WND-1, 281). This is the key to attaining Buddhahood in this lifetime and securing a state of happiness that will endure throughout eternity. A passage in "Run, Melos!" states, "If I am to collapse here now, it will be as though I'd done nothing in the first place."[41]

With my heartfelt prayers, I shared the following guidelines with the Kayo-kai members: "Run, members of the Kayo-kai, like Melos—never doubting your fellow members or the Soka Gakkai or, most of all, the Gohonzon! Run, members of the young women's division!" A life of commitment and deep gratitude is beautiful. Each step in such a life is a step toward victory and happiness.

Today, former Kayo-kai members are still running at full speed on the path of mentor and disciple and working with youthful vigor on the front lines of kosen-rufu as women's division members true to the vow they made during their youth. That's why I have faith in the young women of Soka. As long as it has such committed young women's division members, the Soka Gakkai will grow and flourish forever. The solidarity of Soka women—the members of the women's and young women's divisions working together in harmonious unity—is a source of limitless hope.

Young women have myriad talents. They are a source of encouragement for their fathers, a source of support for their mothers, and a bright light in their families. Later, they can positively influence their partners, become wonderful mothers, and raise successors who have a great mission. In their own chosen spheres of endeavor, they can win the trust of others as genuine Soka Gakkai members and adorn their lives with good fortune, benefit, and success. It's crucial to understand that the young women's division provides the momentum for our entire movement.

No matter how difficult the challenges,
young women dedicated to kosen-rufu
travel a golden path.

Early in the twentieth century, in April 1903, the German writer Malwida von Meysenbug called out to the younger generation, the protagonists of the new century: "You still have work to do and things to accomplish. You still have some battles to fight out. One cannot live without struggle—without struggle and without love."[42] How true this is. We must continue to fight on for our beliefs, striving with compassion for the people, love for our friends, and working to expand the circle of peace and friendship.

Using the example of cherry, peach, plum, and damson blossoms,[43] the Daishonin teaches that each unique entity, just as it is, possesses Buddhahood (see OTT, 200). The essence of Nichiren Buddhism is for each individual to reveal his or her own true and highest potential. There's no need to pretend, to try to be someone you're not, to be impatient and anxious, or to doubt yourself. The Soka path of mentor and disciple is a great path of victory and happiness that will enable you to shine your brightest and in your unique way.

The important thing is to unite with your fellow members and move ahead together with hope and confidence, respecting and encouraging one another, and unswayed by passing problems or events.

As the English writer Emily Brontë writes, "Kindness warms and courage cheers."[44]

The world's foremost
network of young women,
cheerfully
extending their hands
to friends who are suffering.

A young women's division member who had just joined the Soka Gakkai once asked Mr. Toda to explain the meaning of Nam-myoho-renge-kyo. Mr. Toda was pleased with her seeking spirit and replied:

> When you get right down to it, you could say that Nam-myoho-renge-kyo is the life of Nichiren Daishonin. That being the case, our lives, as his disciples, are also Nam-myoho-renge-kyo. It's just as he writes in a letter to Nichinyo: "Never seek this Gohonzon outside yourself. The Gohonzon exists only within the mortal flesh of us ordinary people who embrace the Lotus Sutra and chant Nam-myoho-renge-kyo" (WND-I, 832).

Each of you, the young women of Soka, is a supremely noble entity of the Law of Nam-myoho-renge-kyo. As such, you cannot fail to become happy or overcome any challenge.

The world today is thirsting for the great life philosophy

of hope and happiness of Nichiren Buddhism. Now is the time for us to sincerely reach out and share its tenets and ideals with as many people as possible.

✧

The Daishonin
watches over and protects
the activities of
our spirited
young women.

The French author and feminist Olympe de Gouges declares:

As long as nothing is done to elevate the minds of women, as long as women themselves fail to make an effort to become more useful, more significant, and as long as men lack the courage to deal seriously with women's true glory, the state cannot prosper.[45]

This is absolutely true. Be it in a family or a nation, where young women are vibrantly active, hope for peace and prosperity emerges.

Ella Gandhi, a renowned South African peace activist and great-granddaughter of Mahatma Gandhi, viewed
the Gandhi, King, Ikeda: A Legacy of Building Peace
exhibition in Berlin (in 2003). On that occasion, she
remarked that the more disciples a teacher of peace has,
the wider the circle of people who seek peace grows.
She also said that if the message of the successive Soka
Gakkai presidents were put into practice, it would effect
positive change in the world.

I am filled with deep gratitude for the warm trust and
expectations many thinking people worldwide have for
our movement.

The Daishonin writes that women open the gateway (see
WND-2, 884). There is profound significance in this.

We are now looking toward the year 2030, which will
mark the hundredth anniversary of the Soka Gakkai's
founding. I've heard that the young women of the Ikeda
Kayo-kai—living with a joyful sense of purpose and hope
for the future—are planning to hold a reunion gathering
at that time.

Members of the Ikeda Kayo-kai, may you shine! May
you advance triumphantly! Your victory will proudly

open the gateway leading to the eternal victory of the Soka path of mentor and disciple.

> *Noble*
> *young women*
> *aware of their mission,*
> *winning victory after victory*
> *and opening the path of kosen-rufu.*

(Translated from the May 1, 2008, *Seikyo Shimbun*, the Soka Gakkai's daily newspaper)

SGI Ikeda Kayo-kai— Winning In Youth

The beautiful
unity of young women
working together for kosen-rufu—
a joyous dance amid reality,
a bright hope for all humanity.

Ten years ago (in November 1999), I met with Dr. Jose Abueva, former president of the University of the Philippines, at the then newly completed Soka University Central Tower in Hachioji, Tokyo. We discussed the important mission of women, paying tribute not only to women's intelligence but also to their high degree of inner wisdom. We concurred that if an environment could be created where women can freely exercise their abilities, a brighter future will await the world in the twenty-first century.[46] In today's troubled times, the unique inner wisdom and insight of women are needed more than ever.

My mentor, second Soka Gakkai president Josei Toda, declared: "Humanity must change its course by focusing on the happiness of women. It is crucial, therefore, that young women possess a sound life philosophy and forge a vigorous life force that will allow them to be undefeated by any onslaught of karma."

My wife and I are especially overjoyed to see that our young women's division members everywhere are striving cheerfully and energetically to expand the alliance of the SGI Ikeda Kayo-kai.

> *Millions*
> *of young women*
> *across the globe*
> *advancing toward happiness*
> *signals the dawn of a new age.*

Some admirable members of the young women's division International Group in Japan sent me a wonderful collection of sayings from around the world, which they translated. Among the collection is a beautiful maxim from Kazakhstan in Central Asia, "Flowers are the beauty of the earth, and young women are the flowers of the people."[47]

Today, our young women's division members are reaching out to others in dialogue all over the world. In India, the land of Buddhism's origin, the young women's division has grown fivefold in the last seven years. I have also received inspiring news from Argentina that the attendance of young women's division members at discussion meetings has doubled in the last year.

Nichiren Daishonin writes, "Women, *myo* [the mystic truth], and Shakyamuni are identical" (GZ, 842),[48] meaning that women themselves embody the wondrous Mystic Law and the supremely noble life-state of Buddhahood.

Hope and joy are born when one courageous young woman stands up with firm faith. Be it in the home, the workplace, or the community, wherever there are wise women who brim with the good fortune and benefit gained through practicing Nichiren Buddhism, the bright light of lasting prosperity will shine on into the future.

> *In order to build*
> *a life of happiness,*
> *make your heart shine*

through dedicating
your youth to truth and justice.

All people experience problems and hardships in their youth. No life is without problems. In fact, our problems help us grow. Without challenge, there can be no true happiness; at best, one would have a shallow, illusory happiness lacking any solid or lasting foundation.

Nichiren Daishonin proclaims, "A woman who embraces the lion king of the Lotus Sutra never fears any of the beasts of hell or of the realms of hungry spirits and animals" (WND-I, 949). Nichiren Buddhism enables women to lead strong and triumphant lives, no matter what misfortune they experience, no matter how oppressive the society in which they live.

In times of sorrow, adversity, or suffering, never forget the hope-filled Buddhist principles of "earthly desires are enlightenment" and "changing poison into medicine." Just take that courageous first step and make your way forward, ever forward, together with me and with your fellow members. That is the hallmark of noble champions of youth who possess a lofty mission. Such women are admired by all as experts in the art of happiness with beautiful smiles. They refuse to be defeated by anything and warmly embrace and encourage everyone—like our noble women's division members, the mothers of Soka.

On May 5, 1979, at the Kanagawa Culture Center in Yokohama, overlooking the blue sea, I wrote a calligraphy featuring the word *justice,* inscribing in its bottom right-hand corner the words "I carry the banner of justice alone." I said to the youth division leaders with me on that occasion: "In this time of adversity, I will foster the youth. For in a turbulent age, we must place our trust squarely in the power of youth." I will especially never forget the eyes of the young women there that day, which shone with a profound pledge.

The Soka Gakkai and the SGI have triumphed over every challenge through the sincere prayers of women who have shared my spirit and advanced alongside me. The commitment of these dedicated pioneers has been inherited by our current Ikeda Kayo-kai members all around the world.

Dr. Margarita Vorobyova-Desyatovskaya of the Institute of Oriental Studies of the Russian Academy of Sciences in St. Petersburg is a leading scholar of the Lotus Sutra. In praise of the efforts of SGI members, she has said: "The voice of the Buddha continues to speak to us today as the voices of those who have correctly inherited his teaching."[49] Wherever the cheerful and invigorating voices of our young women's division members resound, the gateway to the everlasting victory of kosen-rufu is buoyantly opened still further.

> *You, the noble young women,*
> *who embody the mentor-disciple spirit,*
> *may you accumulate eternal*
> *good fortune and benefit,*
> *becoming "millionaires in happiness."*

(Translated from the May 2009 *Daibyakurenge*, the Soka Gakkai's monthly study journal)

The Vow of the Ikeda Kayo-kai

By Shin'ichi Yamamoto

> *Members of the Ikeda Kayo-kai—*
> *be the pioneering young women*
> *of kosen-rufu,*
> *confident that your meaningful youth*
> *will bring you eternal benefit.*

Every day I receive letters from Ikeda Kayo-kai members throughout Japan and the world reporting on their wonderful growth and development. I feel as if a brilliant gateway to victory is opening wide for our Soka movement in the twenty-first century. Both my wife and I are truly delighted.

The Kayo-kai members, dedicated young women who uphold the Mystic Law, are vibrantly active around the globe—including in the Americas: the United States,

Canada, Mexico, Panama, Brazil, Argentina, Peru, and Chile; in Oceania: Australia, New Zealand, and Micronesia; in Europe: France, Italy, the United Kingdom, Germany, the Netherlands, and Slovenia; in Asia: South Korea, Hong Kong, Taiwan, the Philippines, India, Malaysia, Singapore, Thailand, Indonesia, and Cambodia; and in Africa: the Côte d'Ivoire, Cameroon, and Zambia.

This is, of course, by no means a complete list. In some countries, when the group was launched, there were only a handful of young women's division members. Nevertheless, they all stood up determined to personally contribute to creating happy and peaceful communities. This spirit of the Kayo-kai is extremely noble.

I also recently received some good news from the United States. SGI-USA Young Women's Leader Vinessa Shaw was interviewed on a popular public radio program called *Interfaith Voices* (on May 14, 2009). In the interview, she spoke refreshingly about the great satisfaction she derives from her work as a film actress, sharing how practicing Nichiren Buddhism and having a mentor in life serve as tremendous sources of strength and inspiration each day. The program received a very positive response from listeners, with many saying they were impressed and encouraged by her words.

Nichiren Daishonin writes, "When the sun rises in the eastern sector of the sky, then all the skies over the great continent of Jambudvipa in the south [i.e., the entire world] will be illuminated" (WND-1, 169). Similarly, the sun rising in the hearts of our intrepid Kayo-kai members everywhere will illuminate the communities and countries in which they live.

In Japan, the recent formation of the second "class" of the Ikeda Kayo-kai (in March 2009) has brought with it a fresh wave of energy and joy.

> *Be strong*
> *and beautiful,*
> *my beloved young women's division members,*
> *and today again accumulate*
> *everlasting good fortune.*

On February 18 this year (2009), I first heard the original draft for the young women's new song, "The Vow of the Ikeda Kayo-kai," which is now being sung throughout Japan and also [in translation] in other parts of the world. I thought it was a fine song and that its writing team had done a commendable job. But I knew that they could do even better—that, with the challenging spirit of the Kayo-kai, they could easily go beyond what they had achieved so far and produce not just a good song but a great one that would live on for generations. This is because I truly believe in the potential of these young leaders I had fostered. I shared these thoughts at the women's division and young women's division executive conference that day.

United in purpose, the Kayo-kai songwriting team members eagerly set themselves to the challenge once more. Fueled by Nam-myoho-renge-kyo and passionate life force, they infused the lyrics with a deeper vow, an even more profound commitment.

Mentors believe in their disciples. It is precisely because of their immense faith in and hopes for their disciples that they are not easy on them, that they train them thoroughly and are strict with them. Disciples who respond wholeheartedly to their mentor's belief in them can bring forth immeasurable power and ability. This is the rhythm of mentor and disciple. It is a symphony of victory.

I heard the new version of the Kayo-kai song two days later. It had been completely rewritten and brimmed with vibrant joy. [*The following is a literal translation of the Japanese lyrics for the song's third verse.*]

Now, together with our mentor,
committed to truth and justice,
we will build an age of peace
for all women around the world,
striving brightly side by side
with our Kayo-kai sisters.
"Ikeda Kayo-kai, dance as flowers of mission!"—
heeding this call, we will joyfully fulfill
the vow of the Kayo-kai, a vow of gratitude.

In *The Record of the Orally Transmitted Teachings,* the Daishonin states: "Great joy [is what] one experiences when one understands for the first time that one's mind from the very beginning has been the Buddha. Nam-myoho-renge-kyo is the greatest of all joys" (OTT, 211–12); and "Joy means both oneself and others possessing wisdom and compassion" (OTT, 146). The joy taught in Buddhism is more than ordinary joy. It is to know our infinitely noble mission as people who have been Buddhas from the very beginning. It is to stand up courageously alongside our fellow members, overflowing with the joy of having encountered the Mystic Law, which enables all people to attain enlightenment.

The revised lyrics for the Kayo-kai song beautifully captured the joy of a life dedicated to that mission as well as the lofty bonds of shared commitment. Listening to them, I could feel the young women's bright, spirited resolve to never be defeated by any hardship and to start anew with fresh determination.

I was delighted with the results: "It's fabulous! Perfect!" Smiling, my wife agreed, "It's very good—cheerful, invigorating, and easy to remember."

With English and Mandarin Chinese versions of the song now also completed, the hopeful melody of "The Vow of the Ikeda Kayo-kai" continues to spread around the globe.

❀

Never forgetting
the importance
of perseverance and faith,
attain happiness,
ascending the jeweled summit.

My mentor, second Soka Gakkai president Josei Toda, frequently talked about the importance of changing the course of women's history because, for far too long, far too many women had been tossed about by the vicissitudes of the times and left to weep over cruel and bitter fates. Speaking in a warmhearted, fatherly manner to a group of young women, he once said: "I want to see you all become happy without fail. I want you to come to me in five or ten years and report to me, 'Sensei, I have become so happy!'" My wife and I share the exact same sentiment. Or rather, our pledge and our sincerest determination is that every single member of the young women's division, without exception, will become happy.

It's also important for all men's and women's division leaders, as elders in the Soka family, to pray for the happiness of the young women's division. Let us cherish, encourage, support, and cheer on the young women of our organization.

In the early days of the Soka Gakkai, there was a woman who, after graduating as a top leader of the young women's division, went on to become a leader in the women's division. Though having the good fortune to receive guidance directly from Mr. Toda, she later created disunity in the women's division and was spiteful and malicious to her juniors. A year after Mr. Toda's death, the young women's division worked hard to compose a new divisional song as a symbol of their resolve to make a fresh start. However, this woman coldly said that their song could never be an official song of the young women's division. She insisted that only the song that she had helped write as a young women's leader could ever be regarded as the true young women's division song.[50]

Just as Mr. Toda had predicted with sharp and penetrating insight, this woman and her husband—a men's leader who had no sense of appreciation or gratitude—became consumed with jealousy and resentment and went on to disrupt the harmony of the members, attack the Soka Gakkai, and ultimately abandon their faith. As the Daishonin writes, "The cart that overturns on the road ahead is a warning to the one behind" (WND-1, 497).

Fortunately, today, the members of the women's and young women's divisions enjoy a beautiful unity as sisters working together and advancing toward a common goal.

By the way, newly appointed Soka Gakkai Women's Division Leader Shinobu Sugimoto and Women's Division Secretary Keiko Kawahara have striven with the spirit of the Seishun-kai (Spring of Youth Group, a young women's training group formed in 1975), of which they were members in their youth. They have expressed their sincere wish to be the kind of women's division members who always encourage and support their juniors in the young women's division, in the same way that they were once encouraged and supported by many of their seniors in faith in the women's division.

Like beautiful flowers,
like the morning sun,
the members of the Kayo-kai
carry out their profound vow,
the mentor watching on.

The original Kayo-kai—the young women's group that was the forerunner of today's Ikeda Kayo-kai—was founded in the autumn of 1952, and its members were personally trained by Mr. Toda. At his instruction, my wife, though already a women's division member [having married in May 1952 and graduated from the young women's division], was included as a member of this honored group.

Incidentally, my wife was one of the original seventy-four members making up the young women's division when it was founded on July 19, 1951. She also gave her all in the February campaign of 1952 in Kamata Chapter as a group leader—the equivalent of a young women's district or chapter leader today. While holding down a full-time job at a bank and showing actual proof of faith in her workplace, she strove tirelessly to help solidify the foundation for the young women's division in the early days of our movement.

❖

In December 1951, some five months after the division had been founded, my wife made a study presentation on the topic of "Work and Faith" at a young women's meeting attended by Mr. Toda. She discussed the following passage from the Daishonin's writing "The Bow and Arrow" [a letter he addressed to the lay nun Toki]:

> It is the power of the bow that determines the flight of the arrow, the might of the dragon that controls the movement of the clouds,[51] and the strength of the wife that guides the actions of her husband. In the same way, it is your support that has enabled [your husband] Toki [Jonin] to visit me here now. We know the fire by its smoke, discern the nature of the dragon by the rain, and recognize the wife by observing her husband. Thus, meeting here at this moment with Toki, I feel as if I were seeing you. (WND-1, 656)

This passage indicates how important women are in their family, their community, and society at large.

In her presentation, my wife said: "The Daishonin's words urge us to awaken to the fact that we women are actually the driving force of the Soka Gakkai, which is powering ahead to kosen-rufu, and have an important role to play. It makes me keenly feel just how crucial we are in this endeavor."

She also cited Mr. Toda's words, "If you neglect your responsibilities at home and at work, you are not correctly upholding the Daishonin's Buddhism," and added, "We need to fulfill our individual responsibilities and win the respect of others, becoming indispensable in our places of work."

She also said that in order not to lose sight of our key goal of kosen-rufu and make poor judgments as a result, it was vital that we always take action based on faith in the Gohonzon and that we sincerely trust and believe in Mr. Toda. When she was finished, Mr. Toda smiled and applauded her presentation.

The way of mentor and disciple is the ultimate path of human life and the direct course to victory in life. My wife, a pioneer of the young women's division, joyously fulfilled her vow as a Kayo-kai member, a vow based on profound gratitude.

Embraced by
the entire universe,
live out your lives joyfully,

assured of the benefits
of the Mystic Law.

The United Nations has designated this year (2009) as the International Year of Astronomy, commemorating four hundred years since the Italian astronomer Galileo Galilei first used a telescope to observe the skies.

As is well known, Galileo was persecuted and unjustly tried, his landmark findings attacked by those who were envious of his greatness. Galileo's beloved eldest daughter, Maria Celeste Galilei, supported and prayed for her father more than anyone else during his troubles. She was confident that the "prayers of a pious daughter could outweigh even the protection of great personages."[52]

She sent letters to her father from the outskirts of Florence while he faced his struggles in Rome. In one, she writes, "I wanted to write to you now, to tell you I partake in your torments, so as to make them lighter for you to bear."[53] These words surely illuminated Galileo's heart with golden light.

Maria Celeste further encourages him, "[May you bear] these blows with that strength of spirit which your religion, your profession, and your age require."[54] She adds, "And since you, by virtue of your vast experience, can lay claim to full cognizance of the fallacy and instability of everything in this miserable world, you must not make too much of these storms [that assail you], but rather take hope that they will soon subside and transform themselves from troubles into as many satisfactions."[55]

To experience attacks and abuse while struggling for truth and justice yet never be defeated is the mark of an unsurpassed life.

Thirty years ago (in 1979), in the turbulent times following my resignation as the third president of the Soka Gakkai, I received numerous letters of solidarity from young women's division members affirming their pure-hearted commitment to continue struggling alongside me for kosen-rufu. My wife and I have preserved each of those letters as precious treasures of the Soka movement.

❀

Buoyantly
living your youth
to the full,
overcome your difficulties
as princesses of victory.

One of the books that the original Kayo-kai members studied with Mr. Toda back in the 1950s was *Little Women.* The author, Louisa May Alcott, remarked with humorous irony in her diary when she was young: "I think disappointment must be good for me, I get so much of it, and the constant thumping Fate gives me may be a mellowing process, so I shall be a ripe and sweet old pippin [apple] before I die."[56] Youth is a time fraught with countless problems and challenges. Society, too, is always changing. There are certain to be times when you find yourself at an impasse in your job. You may fall ill. Personal relationships may at times also be difficult. Sometimes you might be envious of others. And there might be days when you feel like crying out of frustration or resentment.

In *The Record of the Orally Transmitted Teachings,* the Daishonin, however, speaks of "burning the firewood of earthly desires [and] summoning up the wisdom fire of bodhi or enlightenment" (OTT, 11). In other words, the essence of Nichiren Buddhism is that earthly desires lead to enlightenment. Without suffering, without problems, we cannot bring forth the wisdom of enlightenment, we cannot grow, and we cannot attain Buddhahood.

A woman who upholds this supreme philosophy of hope that is Nichiren Buddhism can advance with optimism and self-confidence at all times, even when things don't go as planned.

The Daishonin teaches us: "Suffer what there is to suffer, enjoy what there is to enjoy. Regard both suffering and joy as facts of life, and continue chanting Nam-myoho-renge-kyo, no matter what happens" (WND-1, 681). When you are suffering, please chant Nam-myoho-renge-kyo just as you are, suffering and all. A path forward is certain to open. With faith, there is absolutely no hardship or deadlock that we cannot overcome.

Many people let their youth go to waste, self-absorbed with their own petty problems and dramas. In contrast, those who spend their youth working energetically to realize the great vow of kosen-rufu find that the bigger the challenges they face, the more expansive their life-condition becomes and the greater the good fortune they accumulate.

Please remember that nothing can destroy the strong life-state that you yourself have forged through your struggles.

> *A life of steady dedication*
> *is fragrant with*
> *the boundless benefit of faith.*

Some twenty-five years ago, I presented the above words to the young women of Tokyo's Meguro Ward who were enthusiastically participating in small study meetings that were held each month by the young women's division in Japan.

And about twenty years ago, I sent the following words of encouragement to young women's division members in Tokyo's Setagaya Ward:

> *Those who persevere in faith*
> *are guaranteed happiness.*
> *This is the teaching of the Lotus Sutra*
> *and the Daishonin's Buddhism.*

Those young women of Meguro and Setagaya wards have now grown into outstanding women's division members, and from time to time they write to me about their victories and how happy they've become.

Taking sincere action when the opportunity presents itself can bring about wonderful future results.

❦

> *As the sunshine of kosen-rufu,*
> *may you cheerfully win*
> *victory after victory,*
> *the Buddhas and heavenly deities*
> *protecting and watching over you.*

The Canadian author L. M. Montgomery is best known for her Anne series of novels, the most famous of which is *Anne of Green Gables*. The main character, Anne, is an active, socially engaged young woman. In one of the novels, she and the other young people in Avonlea, the novel's setting, form a "village improvement society" with the aim of bettering their community. Their first project is to repair and paint the village's public hall, and they start by visiting the homes of all the residents to ask for financial contributions for this undertaking.[57]

Anne and her best friend, Diana, begin by going to a street where many difficult and unfriendly people live. When Diana says it's the very worst road they could start with, Anne replies cheerily, "That is why I chose it."[58]

Taking on the hardest challenge is the way to achieve fresh victory.

Anne and Diana speak to one resident after another. Some of them refuse to listen and coldly shut the door on them, while others pretend not to be at home. Some, however, receive them with unexpected warmth and kindness.

It is impossible to know what people are like without talking to them.

At Anne's urging, the two young women then visit the home of a family that has just had a baby. Although the man of the house is known to be rather unfriendly, in his joy at the baby's birth he happily gives them a donation.

It is a mistake to prejudge people based on rumors

and preconceived notions. Of course, the world is a dangerous place, so it's important to recognize ill-intentioned people and stay away from them.

On a related note, I hope that our young women's division members in particular will remind one another not to be too late returning home after meeting at night. Please act with wisdom and don't make your parents worry. I want you to enjoy good health and to be absolutely safe and sound.

The important thing is to make all of your experiences—both pleasant and unpleasant—a powerful springboard to propel you forward as you joyfully walk the path of youth. At the same time, I hope you will continue to talk to others about our inspiring aims and ideals. If you courageously take action to advance the cause of good, you will definitely effect change. If you speak sincerely to others, you will increase understanding and create new friends and allies. Moreover, actions based on wholehearted prayer always bring forth protection by the positive forces of the universe. Those who refuse to give up win out in the end.

Every day, the young women of the Ikeda Kayo-kai are writing an immortal story of youth unsurpassed in all the world.

The network of youthful victory of the Ikeda Kayo-kai has begun to dispel the dark clouds hanging over society and to illuminate our troubled century with the light of hope.

The SGI Ikeda Kayo-kai Apricot Tree, which was planted at the Makiguchi Memorial Garden in Hachioji, Tokyo (on April 22, 2009), will continue to grow tall and strong with every passing year, together with all of you.

I hope you will continue your lively, high-spirited march toward victory, joyously singing the Kayo-kai song. My wife and I are praying for you and watching over you, your bright smiles our greatest joy and reward.

In closing, I would like to present to all our noble Ikeda Kayo-kai members around the world a poem that I once presented to the Tokyo Region young women's division:

> *If you are courageous*
> *in faith,*
> *there is nothing to fear,*
> *for the entire world*
> *is a Buddha land.*

(Translated from the June 3, 2009, *Seikyo Shimbun,* the Soka Gakkai's daily newspaper)

SECTION III

Messages

*SGI President Ikeda and Mrs. Ikeda sent the
following message on the occasion of the inaugural
meeting of the young women's division SGI Ikeda
Kayo-kai, held at the Soka Young Women's Center
in Shinanomachi, Tokyo, on September 5, 2008.*

Your Victory:
A Symbol of Hope for Humanity

I would like to express my heartfelt congratulations
on today's historic inaugural meeting of the SGI Ikeda
Kayo-kai.

Nichiren Daishonin declares that women open the
gateway (see WND-2, 884). Today's gathering of wise
young women leaders from around the globe represents
the opening of an exciting new door to a hope-filled era
of worldwide kosen-rufu—one that will continue into
the eternal future. The Daishonin, along with all Buddhas and bodhisattvas throughout the ten directions
and three existences, would surely praise and applaud
you with unbounded delight. I declare that there is no
brighter or nobler gathering of flowers and sunshine in
all the world—and in all the universe—than the SGI
Ikeda Kayo-kai!

The spirit of Nichiren Buddhism is encapsulated in the credo, "Not advancing is regressing." Moving forward is the essence of faith in the Mystic Law. We must continue pressing ahead, no matter what happens. This is the only way to succeed and triumph. Those who have stopped moving forward are in fact slipping backward. In contrast, those who keep advancing are the emissaries of the Buddha and manifest the life-state of Buddhahood.

My mentor, second Soka Gakkai president Josei Toda, often said: "Human revolution means continually progressing and developing a happy life. It means becoming happy ourselves and helping others do the same." Buddhism exists for the happiness of all people. The happiness that Buddhism urges us to obtain is not derived from vanity or outward appearances. Rather, it is an indestructible state of absolute happiness realized by allowing the brilliant sunlight of our noble Buddha nature to shine forth and the lotus flower of the Mystic Law to bloom fully in our lives. All of you epitomize this vibrant state of life.

The Record of the Orally Transmitted Teachings says that if we can encounter even just one phrase of the Mystic Law, the resulting benefit will endure for a million *kalpas* and we will be able to polish and manifest the priceless jewel of Buddhahood within our lives (see OTT, 219).

The joyous world of faith in the Mystic Law, the world of Soka, is a source of unsurpassed happiness, health, and victory. I hope that you will strive with wisdom, good cheer, courage, and perseverance to expand this beautiful realm by sharing it with many others, starting in your immediate environment.

Referring to the dragon king's daughter, who was a young disciple of Shakyamuni, the Daishonin notes that the enlightenment of one woman set an example demonstrating that all people can attain enlightenment (see WND-I, 269). In other words, one individual's victory or success can serve as a symbol of hope and inspiration for countless others. Similarly, the tireless efforts that each of you is making to forge friendships and spread a correct understanding of Nichiren Buddhism are contributing directly to the peace and prosperity of the entire world.

During our recitation of the Lotus Sutra this morning, my wife and I sincerely prayed that each of you—the young women of profound mission attending today's gathering, precious treasures of our movement, one and all—will remain safe and healthy and enjoy lives of unsurpassed happiness and fulfillment. We will continue to pray and chant for you with all our hearts as long as we live.

I close this message with my fervent prayer that the

members of the SGI Ikeda Kayo-kai—my daughters and successors who are eternally one in spirit with me—will always shine with hope, good fortune, and wisdom, and be rigorously protected by the benevolent functions of the universe.

Daisaku Ikeda
Kaneko Ikeda
September 5, 2008

(Translated from the September 11, 2008, *Seikyo Shimbun,* the Soka Gakkai's daily newspaper)

SGI President Ikeda and Mrs. Ikeda presented the following message to the participants of the SGI Ikeda Kayo-kai Meeting held at the Soka Young Women's Center in Tokyo, October 26, 2009.

Lead Lives of Unsurpassed Happiness and Victory

We join our fellow members around the world in applauding this significant meeting of the SGI Ikeda Kayo-kai today, confident that all Buddhas and heavenly deities throughout the ten directions and three existences are also rejoicing in praise. Nowhere else in the world or in the pages of history could one hope to find a more vibrant or exuberant gathering of noble young women.

During our recitation of the Lotus Sutra this morning, we earnestly prayed that every single one of you—with whom we share profound karmic bonds—will lead lives of unsurpassed happiness and victory. And we will continue, as long as we live, to chant Nam-myoho-renge-kyo deeply and fervently for all of you, who are so infinitely precious to us.

The renowned Indonesian author Pramoedya Ananta

Toer wrote in one of his novels that woman is the symbol of life and the bringer of life, prosperity, and well-being—the center and source of life, and life itself.[59] This is indeed true. Likewise, all of you who have mystically appeared at this time as members of the SGI Ikeda Kayo-kai are the symbol, the center, and the source of fresh hope for kosen-rufu.

In praise of one of his female disciples who demonstrated great seeking spirit in faith, Nichiren Daishonin writes:

> At the ceremony of the "Treasure Tower" chapter
> [of the Lotus Sutra], the Thus Come Ones Many
> Treasures and Shakyamuni, the Buddhas of the
> ten directions, and all bodhisattvas gathered
> together. When I ponder where this "Treasure
> Tower" chapter is now, I see that it exists in the
> eight-petaled lotus flower of the heart within the
> breast of Nichinyo.[60] (WND-I, 915)

You who are dedicating your lives to kosen-rufu are yourselves supremely noble treasure towers of the Mystic Law endowed with the wisdom, strength, and good fortune of the Buddhas and bodhisattvas of the entire universe. Therefore, the benevolent functions of the entire universe will also surely protect you, no matter what happens.

All of your present problems and hardships actually represent valuable opportunities for growth that will help you become outstanding experts in the art of happiness who can encourage and guide others. By earnestly chanting about your challenges and taking action one step at a time, you can develop and grow as a person and expand your life-condition. Nothing is ever wasted in Buddhism.

Dr. Lou Marinoff, founding president of the American Philosophical Practitioners Association whom we have had the honor of meeting, has remarked, "Buddhism offers more ways than any philosophy I know to activate human potential, to change life for the better, and to engender positive circumstances."[61] He has the utmost praise for our Soka realm of mentor and disciple, which is inspiring people to reach greater spiritual heights and lead truly fulfilling lives. This is exemplified by the young women of the Kayo-kai, a gathering of sisters in faith shining with the sublime light of good fortune and wisdom.

In closing, we would like to present you with some words by the English writer Charlotte Brontë, who refused to be discouraged: "My motto is 'Try again.'"[62]

When the sun rises, all darkness vanishes; when a

single flower blooms, spring begins. That is the mission of the members of the SGI Ikeda Kayo-kai. We, my wife and I, entrust all of our hopes for the future of kosen-rufu to you. We're counting on you!

Joyfully singing "The Vow of the Ikeda Kayo-kai," may you achieve even more brilliant development as the foremost victors of youth. Hurray for the Kayo-kai!

(Translated from the October 27, 2009, *Seikyo Shimbun,* the Soka Gakkai's daily newspaper)

*SGI President Ikeda sent the following message
to the SGI Ikeda Kayo-kai General Meeting on
September 2, 2010, at the Soka International
Friendship Hall in Sendagaya, Tokyo. The meeting
was attended by young women's division leaders
from around the world participating in the SGI
Youth Training Course, as well as young women's
division leaders from each region of Japan.*

Noble Emissaries of Kosen-rufu

Congratulations on today's hope-filled SGI Ikeda Kayo-kai General Meeting!

When I took my first step for worldwide kosen-rufu on October 2, 1960, there were almost no young women's division members outside of Japan. Now, fifty years later, we have a truly magnificent network of young women dedicated to kosen-rufu around the globe.

Nichiren Daishonin writes, "Among all the teachings of the Buddha's lifetime, the Lotus Sutra is first, and . . . among the teachings of the Lotus Sutra, that of women attaining Buddhahood is first" (WND-1, 930). The enlightenment of women represents an unsurpassed teaching of equality and respect for life.

The happy and victorious lives that you, our Kayo-kai members, achieve in the respective countries of your mission will serve as brilliant testimony to the joyous benefit of the Mystic Law and the progress of worldwide kosen-rufu. That thought brings me great joy.

In today's troubled world, more and more young women are seeking a sound philosophy of life and earnestly searching for a reliable foundation on which to base their lives.

In a letter addressed to a female disciple [the lay nun Myoho], the Daishonin writes: "Because one has heard the Lotus Sutra . . . with this as the seed, one will invariably become a Buddha. . . . One should by all means persist in preaching the Lotus Sutra and causing [people] to hear it. . . . In any event, the seeds of Buddhahood exist nowhere apart from the Lotus Sutra" (WND-I, 882). All of you, while still young, possess in your hearts the seeds of Buddhahood that bring forth blossoms of absolute and eternal happiness, and you are working to sow those same seeds in the hearts of those around you. Such a youth of mission is noble beyond compare. The more you courageously talk to others about the Daishonin's teachings, the more people you can help form a connection with Buddhism. Your one-on-one dialogues inspire and spread hope that it is indeed possible to change the world. You are all noble emissaries of kosen-rufu who have inherited the spirit of Nichiren Daishonin.

A life dedicated to the vow of mentor and disciple fills one with boundless strength and joy. My wife, as a proud member of the very first Kayo-kai formed by second Soka Gakkai president Josei Toda, has lived her life undefeated by any hardship or obstacle. I hope that you, the Kayo-kai members, filled with hope and optimism, will continue on the path of great mission that my wife and I have traveled.

I sincerely pray, and firmly believe, that your prayers and efforts, along with your beautiful unity of purpose, will open the way forward for the future development of worldwide kosen-rufu.

I wholeheartedly applaud you, the noble emissaries of the Ikeda Kayo-kai, and your youthful dedication to a lofty vow.

(Translated from the September 8, 2010, *Seikyo Shimbun*, the Soka Gakkai's daily newspaper)

Poems

Collected Poems

1.

To achieve happiness
Walk sprightly in high spirits
The path of the value-creative Soka life
Each and every day

2.

To create a happy, joyful life
Let the integrity and justice of youth
Glow within your heart

3.

For the benefit of others
For the sake of the Law

Adorn your life
With victories in your youth

4.

Beautifully
The noble young women
Embark on their journey to spread their faith
Making each person, without exception
A Professor of Happiness

5.

Blessed young women
Soar
Devoting your pure young lives
To happiness and world peace

6.

In the new century
The young women's division
Glows with the hope of their mission to spread
    their beliefs
Advancing with gaiety and cheer

7.

When you live your entire life
With great hope

Victory comes
It is the path to glory

8.

With beautiful hearts
You march
Young women's division members
You are the world's best
May happiness be yours

9.

Lightheartedly and in high spirits
We engage in the noble struggle of Buddhism
And hasten along the luminous path
It is a new century

10.

Heroically
You run to serve humanity and the dignity of life
You will all surely be protected
By all the celestial deities and Buddhas

11.

Fear not
Our lives embody the Buddha

And all the Buddhas and deities of the three
    existences
Will assuredly safeguard us

12.

Your mothers and fathers
Smile upon you
From their place of eternal peace and happiness
Always praising
Their daughters' vibrant endeavors

13.

With a beautiful heart
You stand for justice
Taking leadership
In proclaiming the Law
Our princess for eternity

14.

Precious disciple
You are one with your mentor
May your life be filled with happiness and
    prosperity
And be enriched with joy and good fortune
For all time

15.

Princess of justice
Benevolent and beautiful
Nobly rushing
To fulfill the mission of the Buddha

A prayer for the health and happiness of the cherished
members of the young women's division

16.

Soka Gakkai
Number one in the world
Advancing peace and culture

17.

Because Soka Gakkai
Has the young women's division
The movement to erase misery from the earth
    flourishes

18.

Stand up
For what is right
For peace, culture, and education
And for your own happiness

19.

Live life with unyielding courage
This is the best path
To achieve happiness

20.

Brightly and cheerfully
Follow the road to happiness
The way of propagating the Buddhist faith

21.

May extraordinary joy and felicity
Bless the earnest and noble members of
The young women's division

22.

We bloom
Whether anyone
Is looking or not

23.

If in our lives
We embody
The wondrous Law
For all eternity
Overwhelming victory is ours.

24.

Like the lotus
Of the Mystic Law
Serenely
You live to bring your faith into bloom in a
    muddied world
O shining princess

25.

The new century
Is built cheerfully and joyfully
By the Kayo-kai

26.

With your mentor as your guide
Seek the essence of the sun!
Seek the life force of the lotus!
The joined hands of Kayo-kai
The world's number one
Garden of happiness

27.

Be wise young women
Who make a contribution to society
With the brilliant wisdom and happiness of the
    Mystic Law

And celebrate the victorious mentor-disciple
     relationship
Of your youth
Dancing beautifully, soaring high in the sky!

28.

A luminous life
A sign of victory and happiness

29.

Radiant youth
Victorious youth
Blessed youth
Indeed, this is the Buddhist Law
This is faith

30.

Along the great path of Buddhist mission
You dance beautifully
Fiercely
O how magnificent is the merit of the princess

31.

My disciples
Who abide in an eternal city
May you shine with the joy

Of the shared commitment
Of mentor and disciple

32.

The talented young girl
Rushes to fulfill
Her noble mission to lead others to happiness
May all the Buddhas protect her

A prayer for the health, happiness, and development
of the young women's student division

33.

Because there are schoolgirls among us,
Our movement will thrive forever,
Spreading the ideals of faith throughout society

34.

How noble
The members of our young women's student
    division
May they be blessed with eternal happiness

Songs

"Cherry Blossoms of Youth"

Ah, the time of the new century approaches
Before us now opens a golden path
As spring dawns on Mount Soka, Mount Soka
Cherry blossoms of youth, yours and mine

Ah, now, at daybreak
Into a whirlwind of blossoms
Swirling, dancing over heaven and earth, together,
        ever together
Glistening in the morning light, cherry blossoms
        of youth

Ah, gazing up at the sky filled with stars
You and I converse—that vow we made
Could we ever forget this path, our path
Hand in hand, cherry blossoms of youth

Ah, our missions we will fulfill
Lifetime after lifetime we gather
In the Eternal City—in full bloom, radiant bloom
Fragrant lives, cherry blossoms of youth
Fragrant lives, cherry blossoms of youth

The History of
"Cherry Blossoms of Youth"

On March 16, 1978, "Cherry Blossoms of Youth" was
announced as a new young women's division song during a general meeting commemorating the twentieth
anniversary of March 16, 1958 (when second Soka Gakkai president Josei Toda, then in frail health, made an
impassioned speech to six thousand Soka Gakkai youth,
entrusting them with the responsibility for the future of
the Soka Gakkai and its efforts to contribute to the cre-
ation of a peaceful world).

In 1978, Soka Gakkai members were embroiled in
complex events stemming from the corruption of the
priesthood. It was a time that can best be described as
a severe winter for the Soka Gakkai. President Ikeda
encouraged the young women to live as youthful cherry
blossoms undefeated by fierce storms, to be young
women who can be compared to cherry blossoms in full
bloom.

The young women responded to this encouragement,
determined to create a song filled with the spirit of their
vow to their mentor, SGI President Ikeda, and symboliz-
ing their pride, honor, and joy as disciples. They vowed
to fight alongside him, no matter what came their way.

Through many revisions and efforts to create the best song, working on both lyrics and musical elements with President Ikeda, the only thing that remained from the first draft were the words, "Cherry Blossoms of Youth."

"Cherry Blossoms of Youth" represents the shared struggle and vow between the mentor and the disciple. President Ikeda suggested that this song be performed at chorus festivals nationwide. The theme of these chorus festivals was taken from the last verse of the song. President Ikeda attended some of the chorus festivals and sang the song with the young women.

In November 2006, the manuscript with all the drafts of this song was given to the young women's division. At that time, President Ikeda stated that the new era of the Soka Gakkai has begun, a dawn signified by the united advancement of the young women's and the women's divisions. He encouraged them to unite joyfully and advance on the golden path of kosen-rufu together.

This song has come to symbolize the eternal prime point of generations of members of the young women's and women's divisions with their mentor over the years. It has been sung over and over, serving as a baton of kosen-rufu for the women of the Soka Gakkai.

"The Vow of the Ikeda Kayo-kai"

To-day, with you, Sen -sei, With e -ter-nal bril - liance in our
hearts, We__ cast a - way__ the win-ter's gloom, Bring-ing
spring: a brand new start. Like a fa - ther,__ you cheer us
on. Un-de-feat-ed, our hearts are one. True dis-
ci - ples for e-ter-ni-ty, I-ke-da Ka-yo- ka-i. We
seek from you, Sen -sei. In rhy-thm with__ your life each
day. To give cour-age__ to all our friends, We a-
wak-en to our vow. Il-lu-mi-nat-ed,__ bright as the

sun, Like Ka-ne-ko's em-brac-ing smile, True dis-

ci-ples for e-ter-ni-ty, I-ke-da Ka-yo-ka-

i. We vow to you, Se-n-sei, With

jus-tice burn-ing in our hearts. We stand to-geth-er, We won't re-

treat, Al-ways fight-ing by your side. E-rad-i-

cat-ing all mis-er-y, With mon-u-men-tal vic-to-

ries. Thank you, Sen-sei! We are proud to be

I-ke-da Ka-yo-ka-i. Born to-geth-er through e-

ter-ni-ty, Al-ways forg-ing on joy-ful-ly!

"The Vow of the Ikeda Kayo-kai"

Today with you, Sensei
With eternal brilliance in our hearts
We cast away the winter's gloom
Bringing spring; a brand new start
Like a father you cheer us on
Undefeated, our hearts are one
True disciples for eternity
Ikeda Kayo-kai

We seek from you, Sensei
In rhythm with your life each day
To give courage to all our friends
We awaken to our vow
Illuminated bright as the sun
Like Kaneko's embracing smile
True disciples for eternity
Ikeda Kayo-kai

We vow to you, Sensei
With justice burning in our hearts
We stand together, we won't retreat
Always fighting by your side
Eradicating all misery
With monumental victories
Thank you, Sensei!
We are proud to be
Ikeda Kayo-kai
Born together through eternity
Always forging on joyfully

Notes

1. Three powerful enemies: Three types of arrogant people who persecute those who propagate the Lotus Sutra in the evil age after Shakyamuni Buddha's death, described in the 20-line verse section of the "Encouraging Devotion" (13th) chapter of the Lotus Sutra. The Great Teacher Miao-lo of China summarizes them as arrogant lay people, arrogant priests, and arrogant false sages.

2. The four virtues—eternity, happiness, true self, and purity—describe the true nature of a Buddha's life, which is pure and eternal.

3. Dharma nature: Also, the fundamental nature of enlightenment. The original nature of the Buddha's ultimate enlightenment with which life is originally endowed. Corresponds to the world of Buddhahood or the Buddha nature.

4. Mahatma Gandhi, *The Collected Works of Mahatma Gandhi* (New Delhi: Publications Division, Ministry of Information and Broadcasting, Government of India, 1973), vol. 56 (September 16, 1933–January 15, 1934), p. 432.

5. Ibid., vol. 79 (January 1–April 25, 1945), p. 426.

6. Substituting faith for wisdom: The principle that faith is the true cause for gaining supreme wisdom, and faith alone leads to enlightenment. In general, Buddhism describes supreme wisdom as the cause of enlightenment. According to the Lotus Sutra, however, even Shariputra, who among the Buddha's ten major disciples was revered as foremost in wisdom, could attain enlightenment only through faith, not through wisdom.

7. Ten honorable titles: The Daishonin writes: "This is what the Great Teacher Miao-lo meant when he wrote that one would 'enjoy good fortune surpassing the ten honorable titles.' The ten honorable titles are ten epithets that are applied to the Buddha. Miao-lo is saying that the blessings to be obtained by making offerings to the votary of the Lotus Sutra in the latter age are greater than those to be obtained by making offerings to the Buddha of the ten honorable titles" (WND-1, 510).

8. Henry Wadsworth Longfellow, "It Is Not Always May," in *The Poetical Works of Henry Wadsworth Longfellow* (New York: AMS Press, Inc., 1966), vol. 1, p. 68.

9. George Sand, *Consuelo,* translated by Francis G. Shaw (Boston: William D. Ticknor and Company, 1846), vol. 3, p. 113.

10. Alain, *Alain on Happiness,* translated by Robert D. and Jane E. Cottrell (New York: Frederick Ungar Publishing Co., 1973), p. 130.

11. Translated from Japanese. Leo Tolstoy, *Fumi Yomu Tsukihi* (*Days of Reading*), translated by Jiro Kitamikado (Tokyo: Chikuma Shobo, 2004), vol. 1, p. 140.

12. Translated from Russian. Leo Tolstoy, *Polnoe Sobranie Sochinenii* (*Complete Works*) (Moscow: Terra, 1992), vol. 57, p. 194.

13. In Indian cosmology, Mount Sumeru is a towering peak that stands at the center of the world.

14. Translated from Japanese. Rosa Luxemburg, *Yogihesu e no tegami* (*Letters to Leo Jogiches*), translated by Naruhiko Ito (Tokyo: Kawade Shobo Shinsha, 1976), vol. 1, p. 290.

15. Translated from Japanese. Rosa Luxemburg, *Yogihesu e no tegami* (*Letters to Leo Jogiches*), translated by Hiroshi Bando (Tokyo: Kawade Shobo Shinsha, 1977), vol. 3, p. 291.

16. Emily Dickinson, *Poems by Emily Dickinson,* edited by Martha Dickinson Bianchi and Alfred Leete Hampson (Boston: Little, Brown, and Company, 1948), p. 340.

17. Barbara O'Connor, *Leonardo da Vinci: Renaissance Genius* (Minneapolis, Minnesota: Carolrhoda Books, Inc., 2002) p. 32.

18. Mary Catherine Bateson, *Composing a Life* (New York: Grove Press, 2001), p. 37.

19. From an article in the March 12, 2008, *Seikyo Shimbun.* Report on the public dialogue entitled "Learning to Learn About Death," held at the Ikeda Center for Peace, Learning, and Dialogue (formerly the Boston Research Center for the 21st Century), on February 27, 2008.

20. Hans Christian Andersen, *O. T.: A Danish Romance* (Charleston, South Carolina: BiblioBazaar, LLC., 2007), p. 88.

21. Translated from Japanese. Hans Christian Andersen, "Warae" (Laugh!), in *Anderusen Shishu* (Collected Poems of Andersen), translated by Shizuka Yamamuro (Tokyo: Yayoi Shobo, 1981), p. 95.

22. Eleanor Roosevelt, *Tomorrow Is Now* (New York: Harper and Row, Publishers, 1963), p. 128.

23. Ibid., p. 4.

24. See Johann Wolfgang von Goethe, *Poems of the West and East,* translated by John Whaley (Bern: Peter Lang AG, 1998), p. 129.

25. Eleanor H. Porter, *Sister Sue* (Boston: Houghton Mifflin Company, 1921), p. 142.

26. Ralph Waldo Emerson, *Essays and Lectures* (New York: Library of America, 1983), p. 349.

27. Helen Keller, *Optimism* (New York: T. Y. Crowell and Company, 1903), p. 73.

28. Translated from German. Johann Wolfgang von Goethe, "Im Vorübergehen" (In Passing By), in *Goethe gedichte: Sämtliche gedichte in zeitlicher folge* (*Goethe Poems: Collected Poems in Chronological Order*), edited by Heinz Nicolai (Frankfurt am Main: Insel Verlag, 1982), p. 671.

29. Mary Catherine Bateson, *Composing a Life* (New York: Grove Press, 2001), p. 94.

30. Translated from German. Hannah Arendt, *Denktagebuch* (*Thought Journal*), edited by Ursela Ludz and Ingeborg Nordmann (Munich: Piper Verlag, 2002), vol. 1, p. 434.

31. Hans Christian Andersen, *The Complete Stories,* translated by Jean Hersholt (London: The British Library, 2005), p. 845.

32. Pindar, *The Odes of Pindar,* translated by Dawson W. Turner (London: Bell and Daldy, 1868), p. 87.

33. Florence Nightingale, Florence Nightingale to Her Nurses: A Selection from Miss Nightingale's Addresses to Probationers and Nurses of the Nightingale School at St. Thomas's Hospital, p. 50; in *Florence Nightingale and the Birth of Professional Nursing,* edited by Lori Williamson (Bristol: Thoemmes Press, 1999), vol. 5.

34. "Run, Melos!" is a Japanese short story written by Osamu Dazai in 1940. It is based on Friedrich von Schiller's ballad "The Hostage" (Die Bürgschaft), first published in 1799.

35. Osamu Dazai, *Run, Melos! and Other Stories,* translated by Ralph F. McCarthy (Tokyo: Kodansha Publishers Ltd., 1988), pp. 114–34.

36. Osaka campaign of 1956: From the beginning of the year, this propagation campaign unfolded under Daisaku Ikeda's leadership. Based on the study of Nichiren Buddhism and individual encouragement in faith, an unprecedented groundswell of faith and practice arose. Osaka Chapter increased by 5,005 member-households in March, an unrivalled accomplishment among its fellow chapters. It was followed in May by the addition of 11,111 new member-households. In elections held two months later, the Soka Gakkai-backed candidate in Kansai won a seat in the House of Councillors, an accomplishment thought to be impossible at the time.

37. Translated from Japanese. Osamu Dazai, "Seigi to Bisho" (Justice and Smiles), in *Hashire Merosu (Run, Melos! and Other Short Stories)* (Tokyo: Ushio Shuppansha, 1971), p. 49.

38. Translated from Japanese. Antoine Mostaert, *Orudosu Kohishu (Ordos Folklore Collection),* translated by Fujiko Isono (Tokyo: Heibonsha, 1966), p. 224.

39. See endnote 1.

40. The Daishonin writes: "Foolish men are likely to forget the promises they have made when the crucial moment comes" (WND-1, 283).

41. Osamu Dazai, *Run, Melos! and Other Stories,* p. 127.

42. Translated from German. Berta Schleicher, *Malwida von Meysenbug* (Wedel, Germany: Alster Verlag, 1947), pp. 57–58.

43. Cherry, peach, plum, and damson: Nichiren writes, "When one comes to realize and see that each thing—the cherry, the plum, the peach, the damson—in its own entity, without undergoing any change, possesses the eternally endowed three bodies, then this is what is meant by the word *ryo*, 'to include' or all-inclusive" (OTT, 200). President Ikeda adds: "This passage confirms that there is no need for everyone to become 'cherries' or 'plums' but that each should manifest the unique brilliance of his or her own character" (*My Dear Friends in America,* p. 366).

44. Emily Jane Brontë, *The Complete Poems of Emily Jane Brontë,* edited by C. W. Hatfield (New York: Columbia University Press, 1995), p. 148.

45. Translated from French. Olivier Blanc, *Une femme de libertés: Olympe de Gouges (A Woman of Freedom: Olympe de Gouges)* (Paris: Syros/Alternatives, 1989), p. 191.

46. Article in November 4, 1999, *Seikyo Shimbun.*

47. Translated from Russian. *Kazakhskie poslovitsi i pogovorki* (Kazakh Proverbs and Sayings) (Almaty, Kazakhstan: Kochevniki, 2005), p. 20.

48. "Oko Kikigaki" (The Recorded Lectures); not included in *The Writings of Nichiren Daishonin,* vols. 1 and 2, or in *The Record of the Orally Transmitted Teachings.*

49. From the foreword to the Russian-language edition of President Ikeda's *The Heart of the Lotus Sutra.*

50. This episode is portrayed in *The New Human Revolution,* vol. 5, chap. 3 ("Victory").

51. In Eastern mythology, dragons were believed to have the power to control the rain and thunderclouds.

52. Dava Sobel, *Galileo's Daughter: A Historical Memoir of Science, Earth, and Love* (New York: Walker and Company, 1999), p. 304.

53. Ibid., p. 243.

54. Ibid., p. 279.

55. Ibid.

56. Louisa May Alcott, *The Journals of Louisa May Alcott*, edited by Joel Myerson and Daniel Shealy (Boston: Little, Brown and Company, 1989), p. 105.

57. The episode recounted here and below is from L. M. Montgomery, *Anne of Avonlea* (Mineola, New York: Dover Publications, 2002), pp. 11–45.

58. Ibid., p. 37.

59. Pramoedya Ananta Toer, *This Earth of Mankind*, translated by Max Lane (New York: Penguin Books Ltd., 1996), p. 312.

60. The "Treasure Tower" chapter here indicates the Ceremony in the Air, which begins in this chapter, the eleventh chapter of the Lotus Sutra. The "eight-petaled lotus flower of the heart" refers to the arrangement of the heart, lungs, and other organs in the chest cavity, which was thought to resemble an eight-petaled lotus blossom.

61. From a dialogue between Dr. Marinoff and President Ikeda serialized in Japanese in the Soka Gakkai–affiliated monthly women's magazine, *Pampukin* (*Pumpkin*), September 2008 issue.

62. Charlotte Brontë, *The Letters of Charlotte Brontë*, edited by Margaret Smith (Oxford: Oxford University Press, 1995), vol. 1, p. 210.

Index